CW00971898

BMW 3-Series

BMW
3-Series

1991 – 1999

Graham Robson

MRP

MOTOR RACING PUBLICATIONS LTD
Unit 6, The Pilton Estate, 46 Pitlake, Croydon CR0 3RY, England

First published 2000

Copyright © 2000 Graham Robson and Motor Racing Publications Ltd

All rights reserved. No part of this publication may be reproduced, stored in a retrieval system, or transmitted, in any form or by any means, electronic, mechanical, photocopying, recording or otherwise, without the prior permission of Motor Racing Publications Ltd

British Library Cataloguing in Publication Data

Robson, Graham, 1936-
  BMW 3 -series, 1991 - 1999 : MRP Autoguide
  1. BMW Automobile 2.BMW automobile – History
  I. Title
  629.2'222

ISBN 1899870 48 2

Typesetting and origination by Jack Andrews Design, Croydon, Surrey

Printed in Great Britain by The Amadeus Press Ltd, Cleckheaton, West Yorkshire

Contents

Introduction and acknowledgements

I drove my first 3-Series BMW in 1975, bought my first 328i in 1996, and exchanged it for a new-shape 328i during 1999. My own money, you understand, not that of an indulgent employer. Over the last few years I have averaged more 20,000 business miles a year, all powered-by-Munich, and I have to say that I have no complaints.

Accordingly, when Motor Racing Publications invited me to compile this *MRP Autoguide* to the BMW 3-Series cars of the 1990s, I didn't need much time to make up my mind. It was clear to me that this project, more than most books I have written, was going to combine real business with real pleasure: if I could live for years so happily with six-cylinder BMWs, I reckoned that writing about them would also be good fun. And so it has been.

But this is by no means a complete story, the reasons for which must be clear. Starting from 1975, BMW's experiences with the 3-Series cars has been one long-running success story, which shows no signs of slowing down. By the end of the century, the range had reached its fourth generation, annual 3-Series production was approaching 430,000, and expansion was continuous. More 3-Series derivatives will follow in future years, and who knows what the mid-2000s will bring?

You only have to look at BMW's sales figures to realize that millions – literally millions – of drivers like what the 3-Series offers them, which must prove that BMW gets it right, nearly all the time.

It was when digging back into history, into BMW statements, and into the sometimes unguarded comments made by

6

BMW bosses, that I came to realize just how deeply the company cares for the 3-Series ethic. At a time when nearly every other manufacturer has adopted front-wheel drive, BMW has stuck firmly to making rear-drive 3-Series cars. When the rest of the world (and that includes Mercedes-Benz, BMW's deadliest rival) was adopting V6 engines, BMW has stuck faithfully to silky-smooth straight-six power.

Even so, although 3-Series cars tend to be looked upon as glamorous, upmarket and somehow exclusive (thanks for that – my bank manager will be delighted to hear it), we must not forget that part of the 3-Series' attraction is the sheer versatility of the range. Rival Mercedes-Benz's smaller saloons might also be available with diesel engines, but they don't have hatchback options, nor do they have such smart and sexy cabriolets – and they certainly don't have such a firmly established supercar/motorsport angle either.

No problem, then – writing this *Autoguide* has been a pleasure, constrained only by the amount of space in which to spread myself. Dealing with BMW (GB) Ltd, who provided many facts and figures, and almost all of the photographs, has made the job easier, too. Without prompt and enthusiastic help from Chris Willows and Alun Parry, of the Corporate Communications Department, the job could never have been completed on time. My grateful thanks to both of them, and to all their equally enthusiastic colleagues.

GRAHAM ROBSON
January 2000

CHAPTER 1

THIRD-GENERATION 3-SERIES

E36 – bigger and better

There was never any doubt that the 1990s-style 3-Series BMW would be bigger, better and (BMW hoped) even more successful than the earlier generations had been. Over the years – ever since the original 3-Series two-door saloon had appeared in 1975 – more and more derivatives had been launched, and demand for them had continued to grow.

The original E21-type 3-Series cars had entered the market with as little as 75bhp from 1.6-litres, and were only 171in/4,355mm long. The largest engines offered in this range were the 143bhp/2,316cc six-cylinder types, but there has been an inexorable rise since then – not only in engine size and power, but in length, cabin space and, inevitably, in vehicle weight. Yet amazingly, in view of what has happened since, the first 3-Series four-door saloon did not appear until 1983.

More than 1.36 million of the original 3-Series cars were built between 1975 and 1982, with a further 2.3 million of the second-generation cars (E30, in BMW coding parlance) following during the 1980s. Second-generation cars had effectively been sleeker, improved and further-developed versions of the originals, but now it was time to start all over again. For the 1990s, except for its range of engines and gearboxes, a third-generation 3-Series would be entirely new.

The first of the new range (coded E36) was introduced in December 1990, deliveries began almost at once, and within months BMW was making more of the new four-door saloons than of any previous 3-Series models. For the time being, however, the old-style (E30) Cabriolet and five-door Touring (estate car) models were to be continued in production.

Bigger, smoother, more sophisticated

For BMW, this was to be the most commercially-important model range of the company's existence to date, for vast sums of money would have to be spent on almost every aspect of the car. Not only that, but design and development work would have to fit into BMW's wide-ranging 'master plan'. Although concept work for

---

Latest 3-Series lines up behind its bigger brothers

---

the third-generation 3-Series cars had begun in 1985, important new models such as the new-generation 7-Series (1986), the revised 5-Series (1987), the Z1 Roadster (1988) and the ambitious 8-Series Coupe (1989) all had to be brought to market before the new 3-Series range could go on sale.

The new E36 3-Series of 1991 posed in front of (left to right) the 02-Series (introduced 1966), the first 3-Series (1975) and the second-generation 3-Series (1982).

Except for uprated engines, the E36 of 1991 was new from end to end – new structure, new suspensions and new packaging.

With a kidney-shaped grille like this, E36 was unmistakably BMW, though the shape was entirely new.

Compared with the previous 3-Series, the new E36 variety was subtly larger, subtly more wedge-shaped and significantly more aerodynamically efficient.

Long before the new car was unveiled, sneak pictures of disguised prototypes showed that it would be significantly smoother and larger than the previous 3-Series models – and that in many ways it would bear a close philosophical (if not actually component-sharing) relationship to the latest BMW 5-Series cars, which had been launched three years before the new 3-Series would go on sale.

BMW's strategy for the new 3-Series was to produce a bigger but still compact car, still with a choice of front-mounted engines and rear-wheel-drive, which offered more interior cabin space (particularly for passengers occupying the

Earlier 3-Series
First there was the 02-Series of 1966, the true ancestor, but the original 3-Series model family (E21) was not announced until 1975, this family of two-door saloons carrying on successfully until 1983: nearly 1.25-million were produced.

The second-generation 3-Series (E30) arrived in 1990, was built in even greater variety, including 'estate car' (Touring) and Cabriolet types. Before the third-generation E36 was revealed in 1990, more than 2.2 million 3-Series cars had already been produced. The final E30 types (Touring and Cabriolet models) were produced in 1994, total production having been lifted to more than 2.5 million.

privately admitted that they might have stuck to the old-type styling of those cars for too long, and that their clientele had been getting bored with the style.

Even before the new models began to appear, the rumour factory had been busy. Not only was it made clear that there would eventually be four-door saloons, five-door estate cars and two-door cabriolets in the range, but it also emerged that there would be a fixed-head two-door,

Additional models to include smoother two-door Coupe

rear seats), and one which was at once more graceful, more distinctive and more appealing in every way than its predecessor. After the old-type 3-Series was finally pensioned-off, BMW executives

which would not merely be a version of the saloon, but would be different in many

For the 1990s, the new 3-Series had a nicely integrated facia/instrument panel. This was the original layout of 1991 – these being the days before 'airbag' steering wheels were added to the standard specification.

This was the nose of the original E36 of 1991. From this angle there was absolutely no way of knowing which engine was hidden under the bonnet. Warning to latter-day owners – the low-mounted driving lamps were somewhat vulnerable and were costly to replace when broken!

structural details and would largely have its own set of body panels.

What was not generally known at this time (principally because BMW had yet to begin building prototypes and had made no

Early proposals for three-door hatchback and open two-seater

premature announcement) was that there was already a proposal to build additional versions – a three-door hatchback type as well as a hybrid two-seater open Roadster derivative.

Not even BMW could be expected to launch all the derivatives of their new

range at once – nor did they want to do so, for there is much merit in the theory of announcing derivatives over a lengthy period, both to give the factories time to settle down their tooling and their assembly methods, and to reap as much publicity as possible from each successive announcement. Accordingly, there was no surprise when the first official sight of the new E36 range was limited to the four-door saloon.

Even before describing the way the new car was packaged, and why it came to be the way it was, I should emphasize one important aspect, namely that this was not just another 3-Series, but a completely new approach to the 3-Series *type* of car. Although it was still to be what we might crudely call, in Ford parlance, a 'Mondeo-sized' car, it was going to be longer in the wheelbase, larger in the cabin and significantly more upmarket and better-equipped than ever before.

Like the previous cars, every one of the optional engines would be canted over to the right, by 30 degrees, not to reduce the height of the engine, but to liberate space on the *left* side of the engine bay for the installation of electronics and extra equipment of all types.

Compared with the obsolete E30 variety, therefore, the new machine was smoother, bigger and more capacious, as these simple comparisons of four-door models make clear:

	New (E36) 4-door	Old (E30) 4-door	Difference (more for E36)
(Dimensions in inches)			
Wheelbase	106.3	101.2	5.1
Length	174.5	170.3	4.2
Width	66.9	64.8	1.9
Height	54.8	54.3	0.5
Front wheel track			
	55.8	55.4	0.4
Front seat headroom			
	39.0	38.0	1.0
Shoulder width (front) across cabin			
	55.5	52.0	3.5
– but : Boot capacity			
(cubic feet)			
	15.4	17.0	1.6 less

When shaping the new car, the designers, as ever, had had to agree on a trade-off, a compromise, even though compared with the old E30 type the wheelbase was up by no less than 5 inches (which meant that the cabin could be stretched to allow more legroom) and the cabin was up to 3 inches wider.

BMW claimed that the entire shell was

Longer wheelbase, more legroom and a softer ride

45 per cent more rigid than before, pointed out that the wheels were larger (and that the ride was softer), that the fuel tank was 10 litres/2.2 gallons larger, and that the weight distribution was an ideal 50:50 ratio between front and rear wheels.

Distinguished heritage! This was the late-1930s 328 sports car. From 1995 there would be a 3-Series 328i saloon, very different in every respect.

Who pulls the strings?

Having recovered strongly from the devastation of World War Two, in the hard times which followed, BMW had to accept financial assistance from the Bavarian government in 1959, yet soon afterwards the Deutsche Bank withdrew its support, and BMW was threatened by takeover by Daimler-Benz!

This was rejected, and refinancing in 1959/60, with hefty loans from the MAN truck concern, then led to the Quandt family taking a major shareholding, which they have retained ever since. From that moment until the end of the century there was never a point at which BMW looked likely to be taken over by any other concern.

BMW, on the other hand, has often been a predator, and has expanded colossally in that time. Factories at Munich (cars) and Berlin (motorcycles) were the pivot for further expansion, which included the takeover of Glas (of Dingolfing), the development of an assembly plant at Regensburg, the transformation of what had once been the Steyr factory at Graz, in Austria (to build engines), and more recently the development of a new factory complex at Spartanburg, South Carolina, USA (to build Z3s and other 3-Series derivatives). Not only that, but by the 1980s a kit-assembly plant in South Africa had been expanded to manufacture 3-Series types. BMWs were also being assembled from kits in Vietnam, and a simlar plant was planned for Thailand!

As is well-known, BMW purchased Rover in 1994 and (after a bitter battle with VW-Audi in 1998) also secured the ownership rights to Rolls-Royce from 2003. At the time of writing (1999), BMW was the largest independent car-maker in the world, with annual production of nearly 650,000 in Europe, more than 50,000 in the USA and nearly 15,000 in South Africa – plus, of course, more than 330,000 Rovers in the UK.

Well over 2 million of this type of 3-Series cars were produced from 1982 to the early 1990s. The new E36 variety would have a longer wheelbase, more cabin space and a completely different style.

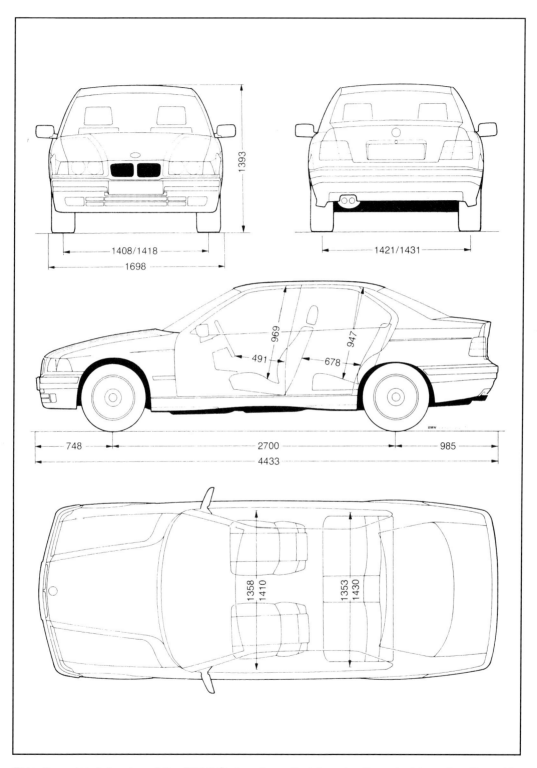

This dimensional drawing of the E36 3-Series shows that the wheelbase had been lengthened to 106.3in/2,700mm and that there was significantly more space in the cabin than on previous types. This, though, was a compact car, with minimum front and rear overhang and, it has to be admitted, quite a small luggage container.

Smooth where the previous 3-Series had been snub-nosed, with cowled headlamps where previous cars had them out in the open, the new E36 was obviously a wind-cheating model for the 1990s. Catalogue-hunters could tell you which model was which by looking at the road wheels – assuming that these had not been replaced by the owner! Alloys like this were normally confined to six-cylinder-engined cars.

The overall length, incidentally, was up by only 4 inches, so the boot was actually smaller than before. BMW's view was that too much emphasis was sometimes placed on boot capacity. (Would it take two sets of golf clubs? Would it swallow the weekly supermarket shop? Would it easily accept folded-up pushchairs and strollers?) So they were quite happy to see this container shrink by 2 square feet.

Mercedes-Benz, in fact, had taken the same decision when launching a new 3-Series competitor – the 190 range – in 1982, and Audi had repeated the trick in 1986 with the new-generation 80. As it happens, all were subsequently criticized by the motoring press, and in the case of the BMW, quite vociferously.

The new car's style was smooth, and clearly shaped by the same team which had launched the new 5-Series in 1987. Although the family 'kidney' radiator grille

Wedge-shaped profile provides smoother wind-cheating style

was retained, the cabin was smoother and a lot more rakish than before, more carefully detailed, and significantly more wind-

17

As originally put on sale in 1991, the new E36 3-Series was only available as a four-door saloon, but BMW made it clear that several other derivatives were already under development. Except for the blue-and-white 'spinner' badge, there was never any other badging on the nose.

In the early 1990s, four-cylinder 316i and 318i models normally had this type of alloy road wheels, though bigger, fatter (and more expensive) types were always available as optional equipment. Unlike earlier 3-Series cars, which had started life as two-door saloons, the first E36s were four-door types.

By any standards, the new E36 was a sports saloon, though with many up-to-the-minute safety and economy features. From this angle, the deep front spoiler and the moulded side skirts are clear – all being packaged to help optimize the aerodynamic performance.

cheating than previously. Because the nose was rather low and the bootlid high, there was a trendy element of 'wedge' in the overall contours.

It was only by looking at the bootlid, incidentally, that the size of the car's engine could be discovered – through reference to the model-number badge which, through BMW's logically chosen numbering system, revealed all. A 318i, for instance, denoted a fuel-injected 1.8-litre 3-Series, a 325i a model with a 2.5-litre engine, while in later years a 325td indicated a 2.5-litre turbodiesel-engined car. Unless, that is, the new-car buyer had taken advantage of the no-cost option of leaving off the badge altogether: the author's E46 328i was anonymous in this way . . .

Looking at the body in more detail, the front and rear screens were heavily raked – by no less than 61 degrees at the front and

a remarkable 66 degrees at the rear – attachments for the optional roof rack were faired into the roof panel below spring-loaded sliding panels, and there was

Body side skirts and a bootlid lip for reduced drag

as much glass (and as little door frame) as the new style would allow.

Up front, the four circular headlamps were hidden behind clear plastic covers, contoured skirts (in a contrasting hue to

19

It is impossible to tell, from this angle, that this E36 type has a six-cylinder engine – either a 2.0-litre or a 2.5-litre at first in the early 1990s – though the smart '16-spoke' alloy wheels were always a recognition point.

Unless its owner had decided to frustrate BMW-watchers by ordering a 'debadged' car, which was always a no-cost option, it was possible to identify which engine was fitted by consulting the bootlid of the new E36. This, therefore, was a 318i, originally marketed with a 115bhp/1,796cc/single-overhead-camshaft, four-cylinder engine.

New E36 types were aerodynamically smooth in every detail, especially in the way in which the door shells moulded neatly into the roof panel and the optional sunroof was totally flush with the rest of the panel when wound forward.

the body colour – usually grey) were fitted under the doors, and there was a definite lip at the rear top corner of the bootlid. Big tail-lamp clusters pushed inwards into what should have been the bootlid opening area, which did nothing for the already somewhat restricted luggage carrying capacity.

Aerodynamically, however, the new E36 series represented a major advance, for BMW claimed a drag coefficient (Cd) of only 0.29 and 0.30 for the four-cylinder cars, and 0.32 for six-cylinder-engined models, whose engine bay inevitably was much more crowded, and where one presumes that a lot more turbulence was set up. BMW also claimed that, compared with the outgoing 3-Series, there was 44 per cent less front-end lift, and 19 per cent less lift at the rear.

Inside the cabin, the package was right – absolutely right – from day one. Except in tiny details, there appears to be no difference between the 'Job 1' facia/instrument package of 1990, and that of my own 1996/97 328i SE model. Except

for the addition of an 'airbag' steering wheel, and minor changes to the centre console and (extra) fold-up armrest, I could pick out no important running changes.

Right from the start there was a wide choice of engines – from 100bhp/1,596cc to 192bhp/2,494cc – an optional five-speed automatic transmission for the very first time on a 3-Series, and the usual wide range of options and accessories. Even at the top of the range, BMW believed in allowing customers to choose their own special equipment, which explains why radio/cassette gear was always optional (for extra money), as were different trim and equipment packages. On some lower-priced versions even the 'essential' ABS anti-lock braking was listed as optional equipment.

This, in fact, is where BMW came in for a deal of criticism in the early 1990s, for the price at which a 3-Series car was advertised rarely even approached the price at which it left the showroom. By the time more desirable wheels, tyres, 'In Car Entertainment' and other packages had been specified, several thousands of

The E36 had an all-new facia/instrument display panel and centre console which looked nicely integrated, but could nevertheless incorporate many extra fittings. This particular car has the optional automatic transmission (and the instantly recognizable 'T-handle') along with electric window lifts for all four windows. But no steering wheel-mounted airbag at this stage!

additional pounds (or dollars) could have found their way on to the invoice.

Although the new body style could be described as evolutionary rather than startlingly new, there was much innovation in the running gear. Although the range of petrol engines looked familiar (all being updated versions of the old 3-Series types), there was a new five-speed transmission option for the six-cylinder cars.

Most importantly, the semi-trailing arm independent rear suspension had been cast out (but not permanently, as we were soon to find out when the Compact range was announced), in favour of a new version of the complex but very effective multi-link rear end first seen under the short-lived Z1 Roadster.

The new car's running gear was so significant, not only in what it meant to BMW's 1990s plans, but in what it might mean to other future models in the range, that a description now deserves a Chapter of its own.

CHAPTER 2

NEW TECHNOLOGY

Engines and suspensions

Although the new body style gained most of the attention at the car's introduction in December 1990, it was underneath and out of sight where BMW concentrated most of its innovative thinking in the E36 range, for the new car's rear suspension was utterly different – more sophisticated and more versatile – than anything seen on previous 3-Series models.

But it was not entirely new to BMW, for an original version of the new independent rear end – usually described as the 'Z-Axle' (or, in stuffy BMW-speak, the 'centrally-guided, spherical double track control arm rear axle', or more briefly the 'central pull rod axle') – had first been seen under the limited-production Z1 Roadster, which had been previewed in 1986, although not put on sale until 1988.

In spite of the effort put into chassis development of earlier 3-Series models, the use of BMW's traditional layout of semi-trailing link rear suspension had always been a limiting factor on roadholding. BMW, having introduced this layout as early as 1957 (on the BMW 600 'bubblecar') was justly proud of its innovation, and had pushed the system to its functional limits.

But there *were* limits. No matter how much, and how often, BMW engineers tweaked the geometry of the system, and no matter how much tyre performance improved as the years passed, there was an in-built geometry problem. From bump to rebound the combination of a sizeable wheel camber change and the alteration of toe-in/toe-out characteristics was not ideal.

For the 1990s, therefore, it was time to adopt a new system for BMW's passenger cars. Almost by definition, it would have to be more complex, and more expensive to manufacture, than the semi-trailing link layout had been, but BMW thought it would provide a long-term solution to its rear suspension needs. Initially for the new E36 3-Series, and then for new-generation 7-Series (1994) and 5-Series (1995) cars, the Z1 Roadster's 'multi-link' system was accordingly further evolved.

New rear suspension proves elegant and highly effective

To describe the new 3-Series layout without referring to a diagram *(see page 24)* would be like trying to describe a beautiful girl without using arm movements! Everything, it seemed, was to work in three dimensions, the whole installation being integrated, elegant, and enormously effective. The more one studied it, the more impressive it became.

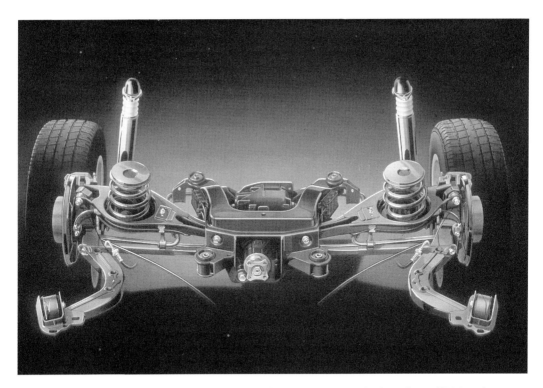

Two views of the newly-refined multi-link rear suspension, which was standard on all new E36 four-door, two-door Coupe and five-door Touring models. From this angle, ahead of the line of the suspension, the sturdy leading links are obvious . . .

. . . while from behind the line of the axle, the mounting of the anti-roll bar, the positioning of the coil springs and the separate location of the dampers are all clear.

The four-cylinder engine, newly launched in 1987, was available in the E36 in 1.6-litre and 1.8-litre eight-valve form, with single-overhead-camshaft valve gear. A 16-valve twin-cam derivative would follow in future years.

Although an eight-valve single-cam engine sounds simple enough, BMW managed to pack a lot of useful and functional detail into this E36 package. The more powerful version produced 115bhp.

E36s with twin-overhead-camshaft, straight-six-cylinder engines, showed off a real bonnetful of machinery. There was space, but only just, for this lengthy engine on 320i, 325i and (later) 328i models.

Plenty of under-bonnet space in the 318tds, which had a four-cylinder diesel engine. The 325td/tds type, with the longer, six-cylinder engine, was another matter altogether!

BMW, it seems, had worked inwards from the tyre patch, studied how Porsche had achieved similar geometry on its 928 model, and achieved a similar result. The whole system was based, and mounted on, a massive pressed-steel subframe which also supported the rear axle casing itself, the whole being bolted up to the steel underbody platform of the new model.

At first glance there appeared to be semi-trailing links, and upper wishbones to control the movement of the rear wheels, but this was to over-simplify the system: it was all much more subtle than that. The upper 'wishbones' were actually control links with only single inner mountings on the subframe, neither truly transverse nor truly semi-trailing, for that inner mounting was several inches ahead of the line of the drive-shafts. Each 'semi-trailing' lower link was actually in two pieces, the forward-facing member being much more substantial, the transverse member having independent mountings at its inner and outer extremities. There were coil springs bearing down on the top of the 'upper wishbones', telescopic dampers were behind the line of the assembly, while ahead of and underneath the differential casing itself there was a slim anti-roll bar linking both 'upper wishbones'.

BMW, while admitting that this was an expensive solution, pointed out that this suspension system gave near-ideal control of camber and toe-in changes, and that it generated a small degree of toe-in at high cornering speeds (and, therefore, as the outer rear wheel was loaded up), to give added stability.

When the car was launched, BMW spokesmen also spoke lovingly of highly-efficient anti-dive and anti-squat and 'predetermined elastokinematic' behaviour' – but all we needed to know, and to experience, was that this was an excellent all-round package, which was to prove its worth in future years.

The front suspension, by comparison, was conventional enough, being BMW's personal interpretation of a MacPherson strut, with a sturdy bottom control link in place of the simple transverse link normally chosen by other manufacturers. As in the E30 series, steering was by rack-and-pinion, power-assisted on all cars except the 316i, which was equipped with a very low-geared manual system instead.

All cars had front-wheel disc brakes larger in diameter and more powerful than before, and at the rear the four-cylinder cars had drum brakes and the six-cylinder models had discs. However, whenever ABS was specified, four-wheel disc brakes came as part of the package.

Engines – an updated range

Whereas the outgoing E30-type cars had been supplied with seven different engines, two of which were six-cylinder diesels, the new car made its immediate debut with only four engines, all of them petrol-powered, all with fuel injection and all with exhaust catalysts as standard. There was nothing sinister or restricting about this, for BMW admitted that additions to the range would be made in due course. [As we now know, by the time the E36 gave way to the E46, no fewer than 11 different engine 'packages' would be used.]

Although the new car's engines – four-cylinder and six-cylinder – were recognizably developed from their predecessors, there had been significant changes in respect of the six-cylinder units: BMW admitted that there were other derivatives of the four-cylinder engine still to come. This is how the two models compared:

Engine	Old-type E30 (1990)	New-type E36 (1991)
1,596cc (4-cyl)	100bhp/ohc/8-valve	100bhp/ohc/8-valve
1,796cc (4-cyl)	113bhp/ohc/8-valve	113bhp/ohc/8-valve
1,990cc (6-cyl)	129bhp/ohc/12-valve	150bhp/2ohc/24-valve
2,494cc (6-cyl)	170bhp/ohc/12-valve	192bhp/2ohc/24-valve
	Catalytic converter optional	Catalytic converter standard

Frugal diesels

There was a time in the 1970s when BMW's image simply did not support the use of diesel engines, but after the first Energy Crisis of 1973 that attitude changed rapidly. Using the facilities and ever-growing expertise of the Steyr factory in Austria, in the 1980s and 1990s a whole series of BMW diesels made their debut: such engines were not only used in 3-Series cars, as described in the text, but were also sold to companies like Ford-USA and to Rover, for use in new-generation Range Rover models.

The first automotive diesel was the normally aspirated or turbocharged 2,443cc six-cylinder unit of 1983, which produced 86bhp at 4,600rpm/115bhp at 4,800rpm, and was derived from the 'small six' which had first been seen in 3-Series cars in the late 1970s. This engine had a single overhead camshaft, driven by an internally cogged belt. For comparison purposes:

323i petrol: 80mm bore x 76.8mm stroke, 2,316cc
324td diesel: 80mm bore x 81mm stroke, 2,443cc

This engine was used in the E30 3-Series of 1982-90, and in 5-Series cars of the same period.

The second BMW diesel to appear, in 1991, was the turbocharged 2,497cc six-cylinder unit as used in the E36 3-Series (see Chapter 2), which produced 115/143bhp at 4,800rpm, depending on whether it was without or with intercooler. This engine was no more than a slightly-developed version of the earlier diesel:

324td diesel: 80mm bore x 81mm stroke, 2,443cc
325td diesel: 80mm bore x 82.8mm stroke, 2,498cc

This engine was used throughout the 1990s in 3-Series and 5-Series models, and even in some 7-Series models.

This was such an outstanding diesel power unit, by the way, that it was also specified for use in the new-generation Range Rover of 1994, where it was rated at 134bhp, and for the mid-1990s generation of GM/Opel Omega range (rated at 131bhp). At one time there was even a proposal for it to be used in the late-1990s Jaguar XJ6 models, but that scheme was abandoned when Jaguar (and its owner, Ford) turned their back on diesel power for such high-priced cars.

The third BMW diesel to be launched (in 1994) was a four-cylinder version of the 325td – in effect it was the 'six', but with two cylinders 'cut off' the rear end of the block, and it shared the same single-overhead-camshaft layout and bore and stroke, and measured 1,665cc. Sold only in intercooled form, it developed 90bhp at 4,400rpm. This engine was used solely in 3-Series cars in the second half of the 1990s.

The first of a totally new generation of BMW diesels *(described more fully in Chapter 8)* was introduced in January 1998. Totally unrelated to any previous BMW engine, this was a family of turbocharged four-cylinder and six-cylinder units with direct fuel injection, twin overhead camshafts and four valves per cylinder. Much more efficient than previous BMW diesels, this variety produced 136bhp/184bhp at 4,000rpm. This time, camshaft drive was by duplex chain.

As before, this new M47 engine was manufactured at the Steyr factory in Austria, and basic details were as follows:

320d diesel: 4-cyl, 84mm bore x 88mm stroke, 1,951cc
330d diesel: 6-cyl, 84mm bore x 88mm stroke, 2,926cc

By the end of 1999, this engine had already been specified for the E46 3-Series saloons, as well as for 5-Series and 7-Series models and in the new Rover 75.

Six-cylinder 2,926cc (330d) types were added to the E46 3-Series range before the end of 1999, and one or more types were also expected to be in the range of engines offered for the new X5 4x4 model.

Having started production in 1983, the millionth of these diesel engines was produced at Steyr in October 1999.

For the moment, therefore, there was no change, like-for-like, to the four-cylinder engines, both of which had a single overhead camshaft driven by a cogged belt, and two valves per cylinder, though the improved aerodynamic shape of the new E36 cars meant that top speeds would be significantly higher than before.

The six-cylinder engines used the 24-valve twin-cam layout which had been introduced with a flourish for the 5-Series cars less than a year earlier. Although the in-car installation was the same as for the obsolete single-cam types – the cast-iron cylinder block was canted over by 30 degrees towards the right side of the engine bay – the latest engine had aluminium cylinder heads with twin overhead camshafts, the angle between the lines of valves being 39deg 30min, which was very typical of modern motor racing practice.

As with other German engines of the period (VW's 16-valve Golf power unit was the same), one camshaft was driven by chain from the nose of the crankshaft, the other camshaft (the inlet, in this case) being driven by a short secondary chain linking sprockets from one camshaft to the other. This was done for noise reduction rather than for efficiency reasons.

Valve operation was by inverted, hydraulic, bucket tappets. Fuel was injected into the individual inlet ports, well upstream of the valve stems, the line of injectors being close to the alignment of the inlet camshaft.

With long inlet manifolds leading to the central Bosch DME (Digital Motor Electronics) fuel-injection control unit, this latest engine looked bulky, though BMW made sure that it was packaged very neatly into an engine bay that had clearly been designed around it. Twin overhead camshafts and 24 valves, in any case, were well worth the packaging – the 2,494cc engine, for instance, was 22bhp more powerful than the similar-size engine had been in 12-valve/single-cam form.

This, in fact, was only the beginning of what would be a continuous development process for these Steyr-built power units. As I will make clear in later Chapters, VANOS variable-timing camshaft control would soon be adopted on these power units, there was a lot more 'stretch' still built into the engines (the late-1990s M3s had 3,201cc from the same cylinder block!), and for the 2,792cc engines a light-alloy cylinder block would also arrive from 1995.

Although the E36 3-Series was significantly larger than the E30 variety which it replaced, there was no space left over under the bonnet, or under the tail, for the designers to indulge themselves. This drawing is of the original 320i/325i four-door saloon, showing the layout of the running gear.

The E36's 'base' engine was this eight-valve, single-overhead-camshaft, four-cylinder power unit, which had been introduced a few years earlier, in 1987.

Powerhouse! Every one of the petrol-powered six-cylinder engines in the E36 range had 24-valve, twin-cam cylinder heads. All were seen as among the smoothest, the most refined and the most capable of any such unit in modern cars.

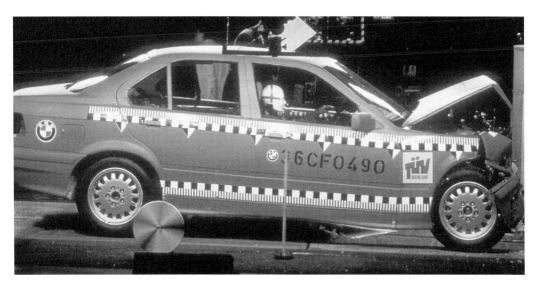

BMW was proud of the crash-test performance of its new E36 model range. When hurled into the concrete barrier at 50kph there was virtually no distortion behind the line of the passenger bulkhead/front windscreen.

Diesel power – a specialized market sector

Not only that, but newly-developed turbodiesel power units were introduced in 1991, first as six-cylinder types, then from 1994 as a four-cylinder derivative of the same design. Although there had been a diesel-engined option in the previous E30 range, it had never been sold in certain export markets, notably the UK.

It may have seemed strange to link BMW, renowned for making sporting and executive cars, with diesel engines, but the fact was that in Europe such cars had been gaining market share since the early 1980s. In 1991, sales of diesel-engined models accounted for 6 per cent of BMW's total output, worldwide, and since 15 per cent of all cars sold in Europe had diesel engines, this was a market which the company could not afford to ignore.

As indicated in the panel *(on page 27)* the latest engines were merely improved, longer-stroke versions of the six-cylinder type which BMW had been building since 1983 – 2,498cc instead of 2,443cc. These were of traditional design, with indirect injection into a swirl chamber connected by a passage to the main combustion chamber, and they easily met both the current and projected exhaust emissions requirements.

All versions were turbocharged, the 'basic' engine producing 115bhp, and that with a large air-to-air intercooler (which was mounted immediately behind a grille in the front spoiler/bodywork) producing 143bhp.

But these were no ordinary diesels. Unlike Mercedes-Benz, whose compression-engined cars were affectionately known as 'Stuttgart taxis' (visit the centre of that city, and you'll understand why . . .), these were still sporty cars. It might have taken more than 10 seconds to urge a 325td up to 60mph, but the autobahn cruising speed was still an easy and relatively silent 100/110mph. When this was allied to a typical consumption of better than 30mpg, the attractions became obvious.

The 325tds, which went on sale in 1993, was an even more inspiring proposition. With 143bhp, and a colossally powerful low/medium-speed torque curve, this particular 3-Series had been put on a par with the petrol-engined 320i. No-one, surely, was about to complain about a 0-60mph sprint in 8.8sec and a top speed of 134mph? With such a package to offer, BMW was convinced that it had done the right thing.

It was no wonder, therefore, that Britain's *Autocar & Motor* magazine wrote: 'Just one mile in the [325] tds makes you realise it is something special, one of those rare cars that amounts to more than the sum of its parts. Drive it a few hundred miles, and you're left with one inescapable conclusion; this isn't just the best diesel car in the world, but one of the best cars outright.'

Later still, from 1994, BMW also introduced a four-cylinder turbodiesel engine, the 1,665cc variety, which was closely related to the straight-sixes, and built on the same machinery at Steyr. Although this intercooled type produced 90bhp, the result was a distinctly sluggish car: it was all very well claiming well over 40mpg in day-to-day running, but few BMW owners could live with a 0-60mph acceleration figure of 14 seconds.

Transmissions

As with the previous range, there was a choice of manual and automatic transmissions for each new 3-Series model. Every car shared the same basic five-speed manual gearbox, all of which had a direct (rather than an 'overdrive') fifth gear. Most models also shared the same intermediate ratios – but a study of the specification panels shows that there were wider-spaced ratios for diesel-engined types, and a closer set for the 328i model which would follow

the earlier models in 1995.

Because BMW had concluded, many years earlier, that they could not justify investing in their own design of automatic transmission, they bought in two types of proprietary automatics for the new 3-Series. All four-cylinder and some six-cylinder diesel-engined cars were available with a GM (General Motors) four-speeder, which was manufactured in Strasbourg, while all six-cylinder petrol-powered cars and the higher-powered six-cylinder diesels were given a newly-developed ZF *five*-speed automatic transmission.

Furthermore, the five-speeder came with a choice of three switchable operating modes – 'E', for Economy, which was the normal pattern of usage, 'S', for Sport, in which the change points were higher and fifth gear was not available, and a position marked '*', for Winter, which was for slippery-road motoring, changing up early, and cutting out the use of first gear to avoid wheelspin.

Evolution

In the years which followed there was a steady, if unspectacular, expansion of the 3-Series range and upgrade to the cars' specifications.

Starting with the 1993 model year (in

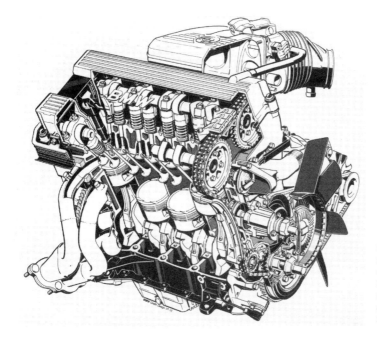

For 1993, BMW announced a new 16-valve twin-cam version of the sturdy 1.8-litre engine, rating it at a rock-solid 140bhp. Camshaft drive was by duplex chain and, at this rating, the 318iS would run and run.

Fascinating to compare the cross-section detail of BMW's four-cylinder twin-cam engine (for the 318iS, this drawing) . . .

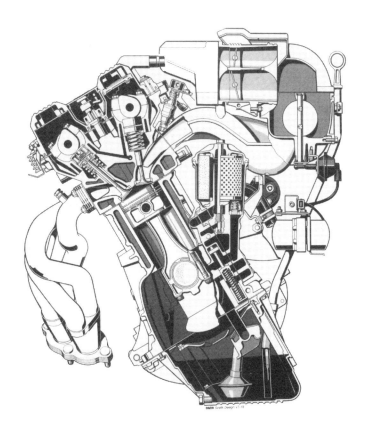

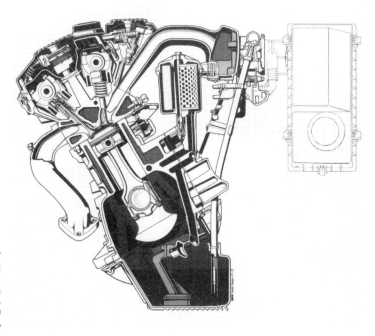

. . . and that of the six-cylinder twin-cam engine (for the 320i to 328i range of E36 cars). Although there are no common components, the general layout, packaging and structure of the two engines is remarkably similar.

Who says that a diesel engine has to look messy? This is the 2,498cc/143bhp six-cylinder type used in the 325tds model, complete with its low-mounted intercooler, which received a cooling blast through slats in the front spoiler.

Can you spot the difference? For 1997, BMW gave the 3-Series cars a tiny but (to them) significant facelift. The new-style kidney grille, slightly more rounded than before and with different slatting in the spoiler, makes a subtle contrast with the 1991 to 1996 variety seen on the right.

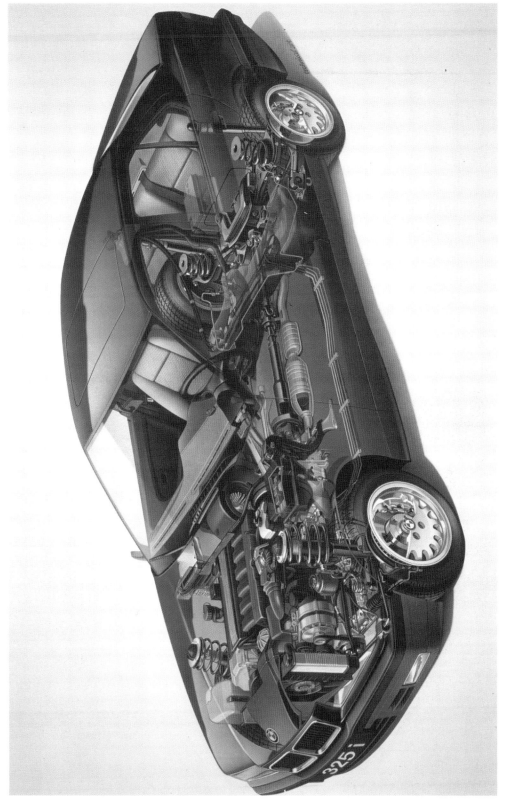

This was the anatomy of the new E36 model in six-cylinder 325i form, showing the new and complex type of rear suspension and the location of the fuel tank ahead of it.

other words, in cars built from the autumn of 1992), ABS anti-lock braking became standard equipment, and VANOS variable valve timing was standardized on the inlet camshaft of six-cylinder engines.

In 1993 (and depending on the market in which the cars were to be sold), 316i SE and 318i SE versions appeared, these having alloy road wheels, and electrically-operated sunshine roof and front foglamps as standard, while in a market move in the other direction there was a 316e saloon – a true 'entry-level' car which had some equipment stripped out, and a much shorter list of optional extra equipment: this model, however, was not a success and it was dropped within a year.

For the 1994 model year, both the eight-valve single-cam four-cylinder engines (1.6 and 1.8-litre) were given a series of revisions which provided slightly more power and significantly more torque – 102bhp and 115bhp, respectively – and this was the point at which steering wheels with airbags became standard.

In 1994, and to combat the threat of Alfa Romeo 155 'Silverstone' models used in 2-litre Touring Car racing, BMW made haste to launch the 318iS/4, which was a modified version of the four-door saloon, complete with the latest 143bhp/twin-cam engine, along with boldly styled front and rear spoilers to increase the downforce. This was a strictly limited-edition model, selling in Germany only at DM48,000 (approximately £16,000 in British currency).

Then, in the spring of 1995, came the most significant engine improvements of all, when the 325i model disappeared and in its place a pair of new 323i and 328i models (saloons and – *see next Chapter* – Coupes) were launched. The naming of the 323i was – effectively, but deliberately – a misnomer, for the power unit was a 170bhp/2,494cc 'six' – a detuned version of the previous 325i engine – while the 328i used a 193bhp/2,793cc 'six', which had an aluminium cylinder block for some markets (which brought about a weight saving of 70lb/31.5kg), and a familiar-type cast-iron cylinder block for others.

The new 328i engine (during the middle and late 1990s, both the author's personal cars used this particular engine) had significantly stronger low-speed and mid-range torque, but virtually no more top-end power, which made the engine even better suited to automatic transmission.

In aluminium-block form, this was the engine some examples of which rather disappointed BMW by suffering premature cylinder wear (and consequent high oil consumption) on a somewhat random

The MacPherson-strut front suspension of the E36 had a familiar-looking layout. The anti-roll bar was tied to the front struts by long drop-links pivoting from lugs high up on the damper bodies. Note the power-assisted rack-and-pinion steering, which was standard on all types.

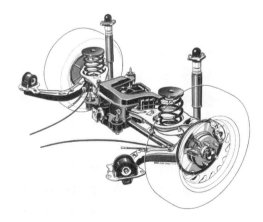

The multi-link independent rear suspension was a triumph of careful packaging, with trailing links, upper transverse links, anti-roll bars, springs, dampers, and an axle subframe all melded together. The object, so correctly achieved, was to provide accurate control of the camber and toe-in character-istics of the rear wheels.

Soaring production

In the 1960s BMW was effectively a two-range car manufacturer – making small-medium 02-Series types and medium-sized 1800/2000 models – but once the six-cylinder-engined 2500/2800/3000 series came along, production nudged inexorably upwards.

The following gives an idea of the way in which BMW's market expanded during the last three decades of the 20th century:

Calendar year	Cars produced in Germany	Comments
1970	161,165	Three different families of cars in production
1975	221,298	Debut of original 3-Series
1980	329,813	
1982	363,000	Debut of E30 3-Series
1985	437,078	
1990	503,087	Debut of E36 3-Series
1995	598,745	
1998	706,426	Debut of E46 3-Series

Overseas manufacture in South Africa and the USA is included in the latter figures.

Same engine bay, different engines – the upper unit with black camshaft covers being the straight-six, that with aluminium covers (below) being the shorter, four-cylinder, 1.6-litre/1.8-litre type.

The subtle restyling of the front end of E36 cars in the summer of 1996, for the 1997 model year, was achieved without any modifications being necessary to the metal body panelling of these models.

During the 1990s BMW introduced a closely-related pair of turbocharged single-cam diesel engines – four-cylinder and six-cylinder types. This is the four-cylinder 1,665cc unit, which produced 90bhp and was used in the 318tds model.

Race cars based on the E36 four-door saloon shell (though using much-developed versions of the old M43-type 16-valve four-cylinder engine) won championships all around the world in the 1990s, but were eventually forced out of the sport when regulations enforced heavier minimum weight limits for rear-drive cars. This was one of the successful British Touring Car Championship models of the early 1990s.

basis. While improvements were still being phased-in, during 1996 and 1997 a large number of engines were exchanged under warranty on a no-questions-asked basis: the author has no personal experience of this, as *his* engines did not suffer.

There were still more changes to come before the E36 range gradually gave way to E46 models at the end of the decade. For the 1997 model year, the first and only front-end styling facelift was introduced, though even dedicated 3-Series watchers found it difficult to identify one car from another. From the summer of 1996, the 1997MY and subsequent models were treated to a front end in which the kidney-shaped grille was a touch more rounded than before, and there was a different arrangement of cooling slats in the spoiler/front end.

Right at the end of the run – less than a year before the last E36 four-door car was dropped – a mainstream 318iS version (not a 'motorsport special'), complete with 16-valve twin-cam 1.9-litre engine was made available.

A long career

By the mid-1990s, the E36 four-door saloons had reached full maturity, though other versions – Cabriolet, Compact and Touring in particular – came along to make an already full range even more comprehensive. In most ways, though, the last of the E36 saloons, which were produced in the autumn/winter of 1997/98, were the same as those which had been announced several years earlier.

Other versions, however, continued to evolve, and were to remain in production long after the *next*-generation E46 saloon was introduced early in 1998.

The 325td (without intercooler, this type) and 325tds (with intercooler) six-cylinder diesel engines were based on the same bottom end as the silky smooth BMW six-cylinder petrol engines, though the block was reinforced and the top end was entirely new. In this guise there was a single overhead camshaft and vertical valves.

CHAPTER 3

ENTER THE 3-SERIES COUPE

New two-door thinking, new marketing

In 1992 the wheel came full-circle. Way back in the mid-1970s the original BMW 3-Series was sold only as a two-door saloon, but such cars were rapidly overtaken in popularity by the four-door types in the 1980s. When the E36 model was previewed in 1990, there was no two-door car in the range – until the new Coupe appeared.

But this is not such a simple story as it might at first appear. Previous 3-Series cars had featured two-door cars which were saloons, with bodyshells which shared all but the vital opening bits with their four-door equivalents. From 1992, however, here was a two-door which was called – and truly was – a Coupe, with unique cabin, back-end and rear-quarter styling.

Two-door motoring – a new approach

As I have already explained in earlier Chapters, the new E36 was not so much a new car as a completely new range. By the time the final derivative – the Touring (in reality, an estate car) – appeared in 1994, there would be six basically different types of 3-Series cars on the market, all the way from humble hatchbacks to super-fast M3s.

From the day that the E36 project began to take shape, in the mid-1980s, a two-door coupe version was already being pencilled into the line-up. Not just a simple two-door version of the four-door saloon, but a subtly different two-door fixed-head coupe in its own right. Unlike some of its obvious (or putative) rivals, neither was it a car

with a cramped 2+2 interior, but one which would have four full-sized seats.

In the event, the 3-Series Coupe which matured was the sort of car which the German motor industry has recently tackled so well. Compromises, if present, were well hidden, irritations such as an over-hard ride, poor ventilation and noisy running gear had all been eliminated, and all the demanding customer was obliged to give up was a pair of rear doors – nothing more.

Redefining the Coupe concept for business users

Not even BMW, however, could have such a new model ready for sale at the same time as the four-door saloon on which it was to be based, so launch and initial deliveries had to wait. The new car, comprehensively 'trailered' by the spy-camera brigade in 1991, would not be introduced until January 1992, which was a full year after the four-door saloons had begun to flood into world markets.

The new car's styling caused controversy

The same, but different – this was one way in which BMW emphasized the style changes between the E36 four-door saloon (left) and the two-door Coupé (right).

– but not in the way that might have been expected. Although this car was built on the same platform, and was being offered with a similar choice of petrol engines and suspensions as the four-door models, aft of the front-door 'A' pillars its superstructure was completely different. The controversy was that for all that, it looked so much like the four-door saloon!

Yet it also looked different – slightly, but definitely so – even though the styling theme, and most of the styling cues, of the four-door design remained intact. Yet here was a car with more heavily raked front and rear windows, with longer doors, and apparently with differences to the bonnet panel and the rear-end pressings. The bonnet and front wings might have looked the same as before, but they were in fact longer, the windscreen pillars being more heavily raked than in the saloon.

Yet those differences were not obvious, and BMW was delighted by that. Critics who suggested that BMW should have taken the trouble to be more adventurous, more radical, in the way that GM (Opel-Vauxhall) had produced the very sinuous Calibra on the basis of the Cavalier saloon, were shrugged off.

BMW. however discreetly, pointed out that this was not the marketing stance for which the new car was intended – and that the new Coupé was not meant to divert too far. They meant to create a new two-door which would be more acceptable to business users (of which there were hundreds of thousands out there), rather than to frustrated sports car addicts – and, in the end, the sales figures proved that they were absolutely right.

Power-operated frameless windows with sealing feature

This was, in every way, a well-thought-out package, with excellent visibility from inside the cabin, and where the larger doors had completely frameless windows. Such features as electric window lifts as

Although the front-end style of the Coupe was almost the same as that of the E36 saloon, the panels were longer and therefore unique, and from the windscreen backwards every detail of the cabin, the glass and the proportions were subtly different.

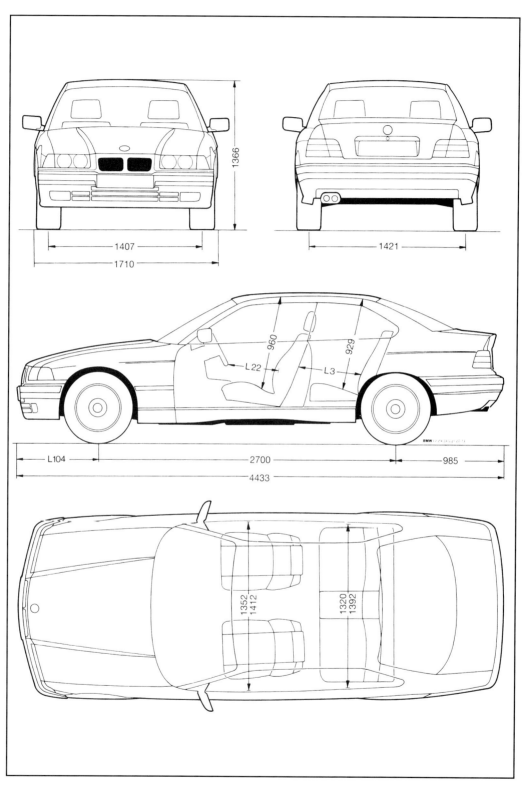

Compare this official dimensional drawing of the two-door Coupe with that of the equivalent four-door saloon (shown on page 16) to see how BMW engineers had made minor, but definite, changes in many areas.

Multi-national assembly

3-Series manufacture, as opposed to pure assembly of parts from kits supplied from Germany, has been most prominent in South Africa and the USA.

BMW started to assemble cars at Rosslyn, in the Republic of South Africa, in 1967, thereafter gradually making more and more components in South Africa for these cars, such that by the 1990s a considerable proportion of the South African-built E36 models was locally-manufactured.

In every way except for minor legislative details (and for the fact that they had right-hand drive), South African BMWs were identical to the German-built types. This became a real advantage in 1998, when 1,000 SA-built E36 318is were exported to Great Britain to forestall supply shortages that were looming at the time the facilities in Germany were turning over to E46 assembly; all of those cars had manual transmission. These cars received such a good reception that other batches were immediately planned. E46 saloon assembly began in October 1998.

When BMW developed ambitious expansion plans for North America, it chose to build a brand new 'greenfield' factory in Spartanburg, South Carolina, where E36 3-Series saloons for the USA market were assembled from 1994 to 1996, and where manufacture of the 3-Series-related Z3 sports car followed within a year. It was widely expected that a future BMW 4x4 (and, maybe, even a Land Rover equivalent) would be added in due course.

From the 1980s, the Steyr factory in Austria had become a major BMW 'powerhouse', providing every diesel engine and a number of four-cylinder and six-cylinder petrol power units – it was the major 'feeder' factory to the main assembly plants in Germany. No fewer than 477,000 engines were manufactured in 1998.

For the year 2000 and beyond, too, BMW had started building a huge new engine factory at Hams Hall, near Birmingham, which would service both Rover and BMW product ranges. These engines were expected to be new-technology four-cylinder petrol engines, some of them being destined for use in E46 3-Series cars in the early 2000s.

standard (where those windows automatically sank slightly when a passenger door was opened (and closed upwards again when the door was shut once again), thereby improving door sealing and reducing wind noise, was thoughtful and typical of the attention to detail.

Continental ski-ing fanatics were covered by the provision of a rear seat backrest that was split so that each or both halves could be unlocked and swung forward to give a long loading area through from the luggage boot.

Running gear

As one might expect, the Coupe was always more highly-specified than the saloons. Diesel-engined versions were never even contemplated, cast-alloy wheels and anti-lock braking were standard on all models (this was nearly a year in advance of the four-door saloon fitment of ABS), while suspension settings were always firmer and more sporting than in the saloons.

In 1992, when launched, there was a choice of three petrol engines and, of course, of manual or automatic transmission. Not only was the car to be available as a 318iS, a 320i and a 325i Coupe, but the 'S' indicated the use of a more powerful, 140bhp, 16-valve four-cylinder engine.

This 1,796cc engine, of course, had already appeared in the E30-type 318iS, and although it shared the same bore and stroke, and the same bottom end, as the long-established eight-valve single-cam type, it had a thoroughly modern aluminium cylinder head, complete with twin chain-driven overhead camshafts and four valves per cylinder.

This power unit, in every way, was a descendant of that used in the raucous and victorious first-generation M3 saloons, and therefore a further descendant of the turbocharged BMW Formula One engine of the early/mid-1980s. In this installation, however, it was a sophisticated, rather than an ultra-powerful, power unit, with solid-

From this angle, there's no mistaking the E36 two-door Coupe from its four-door equivalent, yet every line, shape and contour is different. 'We tried a two-door version of the saloon', BMW said, 'but it didn't work . . .'

Two-door heritage from BMW, with the new-for-1992 car standing in front of (left to right) a 700, a 1960s-style 1602, a first-generation 3-Series and a second-generation (1982 to 1990) 3-Series model, all with two passenger doors.

Not only was the new two-door Coupe of 1992 a visually more rakish and more sporting car, but it had better performance, for there was no 1.6-litre version in the range. Even so, this was a full four-seater.

From this angle it is almost impossible to distinguish the two-door Coupe from its related four-door saloon version, for the front-end styling is near-identical.

Interesting aspect, this, showing the original E36 3-Series Coupe, as launched in 1992. Except for a small loss of rear seat space, the cabin was almost as roomy as that of the four-door saloon.

state distributor, anti-knock ignition control and four individual HT coils. Naturally a three-way catalyst was standard, the entire system being no more noisy than that of other types.

In the beginning, therefore, the new two-door Coupe could be powered by 140bhp/1,796cc 'four', 150bhp/1,991cc 'six' or 192bhp/2,494cc 'six' power units, all fuel-injected, all high-revving, all refined,

---

Refined descendant of a Formula One four-cylinder engine

---

and all giving the car great performance.

Engines – a never-ending story
Although I cover the M3 and its own six-cylinder engines in a separate section *(Chapter 4)*, this is now the time to explain a little more about the way in which the range of petrol engines used in the E36

BMW range changed significantly as the years passed.

Many of these running changes have already been detailed in the previous Chapter, but it is important to realize that the 140bhp/16-valve/twin-cam 1,895cc engine of the Z3 Roadster *(see Chapter 7 for details)* also took over from the original 140bhp/1,796cc 'four' in 1996.

Significantly, an extra 'entry-level' 102bhp/1,596cc-engined 316i Coupe was added to the range early in 1994, though this was no great shakes as a high-performance car, while (as for the other models) new six-cylinder types, the 323i and 328i derivatives, arrived in 1995. By 1996/97, therefore, with the E36 Coupe at full maturity, there were 102bhp/316i, 140bhp/318iS, 150bhp/320i, 170bhp/323i and 193bhp/328i models in the range.

I should also emphasize at this stage that the first of the sensational six-cylinder M3s was launched in 1992, with a slightly modified version of the two-door Coupe body style *(see Chapter 4 for details)*.

World reaction
During the first few years of the cars' production life, BMW's biggest problem was in building enough of them to satisfy demand, for the new models were received

Except for the lengthened doors and tiny trim and furnishing details, the Coupe's cockpit arrangements were virtually the same as those of the saloon. Detail-noters will see, of course, that there are only two electric window-lift switch positions on the console.

with a chorus of praise from many countries. Such was the rush to build and sell sufficient of them to meet demand there was even an unexpected outbreak of poor product build quality at first – something to which BMW readily admitted and made haste to rectify.

Titles like 'the world's best sports saloon', and 'the most versatile coupe in the business' were freely bandied around, and sales leapt ahead, eventually passing those of the two-door E30 model with some ease.

Press complaints that the lower-powered 3-Series cars were not worthy of the type were soon brushed aside by sales statistics. The 316i – really quite a meak and mild BMW – accounted for at least a quarter of all new 3-Series sales: for fiscal reasons, the 318i was also particularly successful, particularly in the UK.

The imbalance towards 'fours' and away from 'sixes' was such that when I approached BMW in 1996, intent on spending my own money on one of their cars, it took time for the sales staff to realize that I was serious about a 328i SE, and not the 318i that they had earlier assumed!

In almost every case there was high praise for the roadholding and handling package, for (as I can personally verify), this was an excellent and well thought-out balance, with great roadholding, a supple ride, inch-accurate power-assisted steering and the impression of a compact ('small', even) car which never felt too large, even

Not only was the E36 two-door Coupe of 1992 definitely more sporty-looking than the four-door saloon, but it had a larger and more raked windscreen, and longer doors to allow easier access to the rear seats.

in extremely heavy traffic.

With grateful thanks and acknowledgement, I am able to quote Britain's most authoritative motoring magazine, *Autocar*, on various of these cars.

To be honest, the entry-level 100bhp/1.6-litre 316i (and its related model, the 113bhp 318i) was not a very exciting car, either as a saloon, or particularly in Coupe form. Though the 316i's efficient shape allowed a high top speed of 120mph, acceleration (0-60mph in 11 seconds, 0-80mph in 20 seconds) was no more than average. But then:

Testers' high praise for ride, handling and roadholding

'If outright straight-line performance isn't the main priority in choosing a mid-sized saloon, then the BMW 316i makes a highly desirable alternative to those less

prestigious two-litre models from the large-volume manufacturers.'

Cars fitted with the 16-valve 140bhp/1.8-litre engine, however, were much more serious and harder-edged propositions. The 318iS Coupe of 1992 had a 132mph top speed, was the sort of car that could easily be cruised at 100mph and beyond, and had overall the sort of character which appealed to many BMW fans.

In some ways the 320i, smooth and silent though it was, fell between two stools because it did not really feel much faster than the 16-valve four-cylinder 318iS and was rather more costly. In marketing terms, this could only be justified by the different tone, noise and character of the six-cylinder engine. In 1995, of course, it was the new aluminium-blocked 328i which drew out most superlatives, with almost every tester in the business agreeing that it was an outstanding package. It was *Autocar*'s comments, I admit, that finally convinced me to rob a personal piggy bank and buy a 328i SE saloon of my own.

Having recorded a top speed of 143mph, with a typical fuel consumption of more than 30mpg (in a 50,000 mileage my own automatic transmission car, incidentally, regularly recorded 29mpg), the testers

When it was announced in 1992, some pundits criticized the Coupe for looking too much like the saloon. In theme, yes, but not in detail. Sales, in any case, proved that this was exactly what the market seemed to want.

wrote that:

'Let's not beat about the bush: the BMW 325i was a very, very good car. Good enough to snatch the mantle of the world's best small saloon at its 1991 launch and retain it against a host of pretenders until BMW laid it to rest . . . [With the 328i] had we not just witnessed it at first hand, we'd scarcely have believed there was this much room for improvement.

'An extra 300cc . . . might not sound terribly radical in engineering terms, but this is all it takes to achieve the transformation that is the BMW 328i.

'. . . it still ranks as the hardest hitting, least compromised, all-rounder on sale for less than £30,000 today – and by some margin.'

Huge demand

BMW, happy to know that they seemed to have got it right, simply carried on making as many 3-Series cars as they could. Production on several sites (including, for a short time, assembly at the new plant at Spartanburg, in the USA) was almost always at full stretch, and it was no surprise when the E36 range became the best-selling BMW of all time by the late 1990s.

Part of this success was due to the charismatic headlines generated by cars like the M3 *(see Chapter 4)*, but much was also due to the astonishingly wide choice of derivatives which appeared between 1991 and 1994. These cars deserve complete Chapters of their own.

In 1992, the new E36 Coupe was available in 318iS, 320i and 325i guises, all with the same style. As with the saloons, only different wheel and tyre specifications (plus bootlid badging) gave the game away – but from this aspect, virtually nothing.

CHAPTER 4

M3 FLAGSHIP

The 3-Series supercar

From the very day that the new-generation 3-Series saloon had been announced at the end of 1990, the world of high-performance motoring had been waiting, fingers and throttle feet twitching, to get its hands on the new M3 which would surely follow. The wait was almost unsupportable, for there was no announcement in 1991, none in the first half of 1992 – and in the end the new-generation M3 did not break cover until the end of 1992, with right-hand-drive versions available from the summer of 1993.

Although pre-launch rumours had suggested big changes, the new M3 arrived amid controversy, for it was so very different in every way from its famous predecessor. Five inches longer in the wheelbase than the old car, wider and heavier than before, and with a six-cylinder engine in place of a twin-cam 'four', it might be a potential supercar, but it certainly didn't look like a racer.

BMW, in fact, always made it clear that the days of racing M3s was over, and that the new variety would be a smoother, faster and altogether more civilized motor car than the original type. Once again there were comparisons to be made with the 5-Series: look at what had already been achieved with the M5, they said, instead of what had rather brutally been made out of the original M3.

Because BMW wanted to start by offering an M3 Coupe as a two-door/four-seater, this was dependent on the launch of the mainstream 3-Series Coupe, which was itself not revealed until January 1992. Seen for the first time at the Paris Salon in October 1992, the new E36-style M3 went on sale a few weeks later. The factory – and BMW's ambitions – had expanded so far and so fast that 150 of the latest type were soon being produced every week: within three years, M3 Coupe sales would exceed the total earlier achieved by the E30 M3 in twice that time!

Compared with the earlier car, the new M3 was understated, more subtly modified, and altogether less aggressively obvious. Compared to the 'mainstream' 3-Series Coupe there were few visual changes, these being confined to a new and deeper front 'chin' spoiler, allied subtle changes to sill skirts and rear valance, and a new type of 10-spoke 17-inch alloy road wheel with 235/40-section tyres – but unlike the old car, there were no bulging wheelarches, no extrovert rear spoiler, and no obtrusive exhaust. Although it sat lower – by 30mm – than the mainstream 3-Series Coupe, this visual effect was rather nullified by the existence of the gorgeous new wheels.

Here was a totally different type of M3 – much more 'small M5' than 'previous M3' – and for the first time it was going to be available in left-hand *and* right-hand drive. Not only that, but it eventually became clear than BMW was also preparing to build the M3 as a two-door Coupe, a four-door saloon *and* as a Cabriolet, too. Not

The first of the six-cylinder M3s was the two-door Coupe of 1992, which was launched with a 286bhp, 3-litre engine. It was, in every way, a smoother and much less boisterous car than the original-style four-cylinder M3 of the late 1980s.

It was typical of BMW at this time that the newly-launched six-cylinder M3 was difficult to distinguish from its less-powerful cousins. The 'M3' badge on the bootlid helped, as did the enhanced spoiler/sill arrangement, but it was the new-style five-spoke alloy wheels which really gave the game away.

Searingly fast, but elegant and understated, made for an irresistible combination in the new M3 of 1992. The deeper front spoiler certainly enhanced the looks, and BMW needed no extra louvres, slots or scoops to keep the engine bay cool.

BMW's sporting heritage was emphasized by the British concessionaires when they posed the brand-new right-hand-drive M3 on the banking of the old Brooklands race track, with a late-1930s 328 sports car zooming past it.

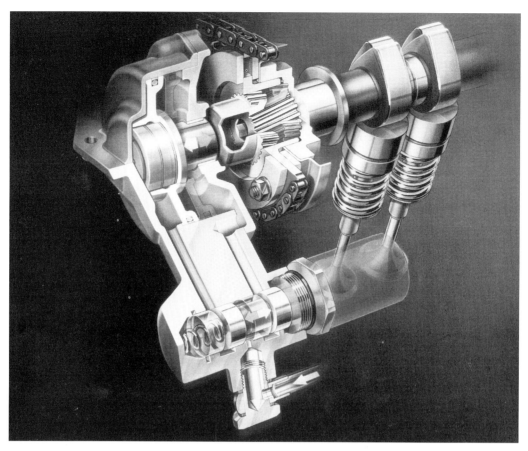

Variable valve timing became a feature of all BMW's six-cylinder engines by the early 1990s, though the M3 was the first to use what was called 'double VANOS' – adjustment on inlet and exhaust camshafts on the same engine.

Overhead-cam 'fours'

Similar but not the same is how we must compare 1990s-style four-cylinder 3-Series engines with the originals of the 1960s. The big change came in 1987 when the modern M40 family replaced the original M10 type.

The very first overhead-camshaft four-cylinder M10, for the 'New Class' mid-size range of BMWs, was previewed in 1961 and went on sale. With a chain-driven single overhead camshaft and two valves per cylinder, it started life as a 1,499cc unit, stretching eventually to 1,990cc in mainstream form. For specialized use in the M3 'homologation special' saloons, as the S14 it eventually grew to a massively over-bored 16-valve twin-overhead-cam unit of 2,467cc.

BMW's amazingly successful 16-valve 1.5-litre turbocharged F1 engines of the 1980s were always claimed to be built around standard M10-type cylinder blocks, artificially 'aged' before use to eliminate all built-in stresses.

The modern M40 engine family used in the 1990s-style 3-Series cars were only superficially similar and differed in almost every detail (including the 'core' bore and stroke dimensions), and were to be built in both belt-drive and chain-drive form).

A new generation of four-cylinder engines was known to be planned for introduction in the years 2000/2001, with assembly to be concentrated in Britain, close to Birmingham.

Wider in appeal than the original motorsport-orientated M3, which had a rough and snarly four-cylinder engine, the new-type car was infinitely smoother, more civilized, faster and more versatile. The style changes, particularly the deeper front spoiler and the new wheels, were nicely integrated.

Cynics suggested that there would not be a demand for a four-door version of the M3, but between 1994 and 1997 BMW proved them wrong. Only the run-out of the old bodyshell (ahead of the launch of the new-style E46 range) brought deliveries to an end.

only was it larger, and heavier (model-for-model, by about 287lb/130kg) than its predecessor, but it would also prove to be more fuel efficient.

Clearly this was to be a functional and 'showroom-friendly' machine rather than transport for 'medallion man'; it was altogether more upmarket and more open-road than 'race track', more country house than paddock. With desirable 328i-style features such as air conditioning, electric window lifts and state-of-the-art sound systems, in every way the new M3 felt like the ultimate, top-of-the-range 'flagship' which it was always intended to be, rather than a detuned race car which was being made for homologation purposes.

For the E36-style M3, of course, the innovation – and the real change of

philosophy – was hidden away under the bonnet. The engine itself was a much-modified version of the existing 24-valve twin-cam M50 straight-six (the smaller of the two six-cylinder families made by BMW), bored and stroked to 2,990cc, and now with a peak output of 286bhp. Although this was 50 per cent more than the *original* 1,991cc capacity, it had been achieved with a 6mm bore increase, but a big increase in stroke, from 66mm to 85.8mm.

The miracle was that this had been done without disturbing any of the costly-to-change basic dimensions, like the distance between the cylinder bore centres, the position of many cylinder head holding-down studs, and the overall envelope of the power unit.

Who on earth needed M3 performance with the top down? Who on earth wanted to do more than 130mph and get blasted by the slipstream? Thousands of buyers, apparently – though most were happy to enjoy open-air M3 motoring in the Cabriolet at lower speeds!

The M3 became 'M3 Evolution' from mid-1995, when the engine was enlarged to 3.2 litres/321bhp and accompanied by a six-speed manual transmission and new-style 10-spoke 17in alloy wheels. At this time, naturally, this was the fastest-ever BMW, with a top speed electronically limited to 155mph, though much more was possible with minor changes to the management system.

To drive an M3 properly you need excellent seats – which were duly provided by BMW in the 1990s. Even more figure-hugging than the optional variety provided on mainstream models, they were comfortable for long, fast, journeys. Incidentally, that is the original type of 'airbag' steering wheel specified on 3-Series cars at this time.

Above the console trim panel, the SMG transmission showed only its gear-lever knob, but the complete change-speed selector assembly was a complex piece of kit. In some ways there were similarities with the Steptronic automatic transmission gearchange fitted to E46 3-Series cars from 1998.

VANOS engines technology

BMW's variable valve timing control system, originally given the acronym of VACC, but later known as VANOS (a German-language acronym), was first seen on 1993-model 3-Series six-cylinder engines, when it operated only on the inlet camshaft of the twin-cam cylinder heads.

Variable valve timing had first been seen on a few high-revving Japanese engines, but BMW evolved their own system for the 1990s, first using it on the 6.0-litre V12 which was specially produced for the McLaren F1 road car. VANOS indicated a complex electronically-sensed control of the timing of the camshaft, where the rotary alignment of the shaft could actually be twisted relative to the crankshaft itself.

This was no step-by-step business, but quite seamless in operation. It was claimed to improve fuel economy, to enhance the torque in the lower and medium-speed ranges, and to further reduce noise. From mid-1995, the 3,201cc M3 Evolution engine featured VANOS control on both camshafts, this feature then being applied to all six-cylinder engines from the start-up of E46 production in 1998.

Peak power was an impressive 286bhp at 7,000rpm, with peak torque of 236lb.ft at a middle-of-the-range 3,600rpm. Here, therefore, was not only an engine significantly more powerful than the best of the four-cylinder M3s (which had a very rorty 2,467cc/238bhp/177lb.ft package), but one which was altogether smoother, more silent, and produced seamless and uncomplaining torque. At the time BMW claimed that the 96bhp per litre figure which had been achieved was the best in the world, so far, for a naturally-aspirated road car power unit.

Peak power, though, was only part of the story, for the latest engine was as subtle as it was sleek, using BMW's patented VANOS variable valve timing on the inlet camshafts, the latest Bosch Motronic DME M3.3 electronic engine management system, a dual-mass flywheel and, of course, exhaust catalysts. Peak torque was developed at 3,600rpm (on earlier four-cylinder M3s it had been developed at a much more peaky 4,750rpm) and the figure stayed well up thereafter, the torque curve being essentially flat all the way to 5,900rpm, so this, and the silky-smooth manners of the straight-six, ensured a seamless, though still tyre-spinning capability.

All this, matched to E36-style suspension that had been redeveloped and made more sporting without destroying the ride (damper settings were only 10 per cent firmer than on the latest 328i, for instance), fat 235/40 ZR17 tyres on new 10-spoke 7.5-inch rims, bigger brakes and reinforced suspension members, made the point that here was a thoroughly developed new model.

The new M3 was higher geared than before – top, fourth and third in the five-speed Getrag gearbox had been stacked closer together – and the final drive, complete with 25 per cent limited-slip differential action, had been raised to 3.15:1. So this was a car which positively ached to be taken out onto a German autobahn and driven really hard; at 120mph, the new car's engine was turning over at an easy 5,365rpm.

This, though, was where politics, and a nod to Germany's 'green' movement, intruded, for BMW, like their rivals, elected to limit the maximum speed to a relatively restrained 155mph/250kph by using obedient electronic controls in the engine management/fuel supply system, though it seemed that well over 165mph might otherwise have been possible. The 0-100mph sprint, in around 13 seconds, felt just as exciting as forecast.

Although the new M3 was also sold in the USA from 1994, for this particular market, where speed limits are lower and law-enforcement officers ruthlessly efficient, the engine was rated at only 243bhp, with a more flexible torque curve and different gearing – so the E36 M3 in its USA version was not quite as specialized as the cars being built for the rest of the world, although of course it was still the most powerful six-cylinder model in the range on offer.

Even in its original form, the new M3 was well-received – more than 6,000 would be manufactured in the first full year of production – and it was obvious that BMW's decision to develop the M3 from a detuned racer into a superfast road car had been thoroughly vindicated.

It was, in fact, a great car which soon

Although Alpina was always an independent concern, its tuning efforts were monitored by BMW and found favour. Here, decked out with special alloy wheels, front spoilers and bootlid spoilers, are the B6 2.8-litre saloon and B2.5 Coupe.

Ultra-high M3 performance was matched by an extremely well-equipped facia/instrument panel. The clues to this car being an Evolution saloon are in the gear-lever knob markings and the provision of four (not two) electric window lift switches on the centre console!

The SMG (Sequential Manual Gearbox) option became available on M3 Evos from mid-1996. This six-speeder did away with the clutch pedal completely (there was automatic clutch take-up from rest), all forward gearchanging being achieved simply by moving the gear-lever forwards (for upward changes) or rearwards (for down changes).

Providing hydraulic and electronic control for the SMG transmission was not a simple task, as this M3 cutaway drawing makes clear.

was to become a great range, for a Cabriolet version followed in January 1994, and a four-door saloon (looking even less extrovert, but with different wheels to signal its purpose) was added in the summer of that year. Whether it was truly comfortable to drive an M3 Cabriolet, top-down, at 120mph and more, was doubtful, but there was no doubt that a demand for such a car existed – BMW sold more than 1,100 of them during 1994 alone, though this represented only 12 per cent of the M3 Coupe's total.

The Cabriolet came complete with an electrically-operated soft-top mechanism, this and other under-body stiffening details meaning that it weighed in at a sturdy 3,396lb/1,540kg. The four-door saloon (first built in June 1994) was only a

---

Factory flexibility means quick reaction to changes in demand

---

qualified success at first – in 1995 only 1,015 were produced, compared with 9,168 M3 Coupes – but as it was visually less extrovert than the Coupe, perhaps this was not surprising.

Accordingly, with UK prices starting at £32,450, the Coupe was always the best seller, for such high speeds in drop-tops always seemed to be self-defeating, while the totally understated elegance of the four-door car did not have universal appeal.

The factory facility at Garching, however, had the flexibility to deal with every variation in demand, and produced more than 10,000 M3s in 1994, which was an amazing achievement, and an enormous improvement on what had previously been achieved. Faced with such figures, noisy diehards who thought that M-Series BMWs should really be for use on the race track had to retreat; 10,000

Racers

Starting in the 1960s, BMW rapidly built up a fine reputation in Touring Car racing, first with four-cylinder saloons, and later with increasingly special two-door Coupes. In the 1970s, the BMW-versus-Ford battles made many headlines.

By the 1990s, most front-line Touring Car racing championships were run to a new 'Super Touring' formula, which required cars, of a certain minimum length and weight, to use naturally-aspirated 2.0-litre engines, electronically limited to 8,500rpm. By the mid-1990s, that formula had also been extended to specify four-door or five-door bodyshells.

In the early years, 3-Series BMWs were ideal for such sport, and at one time the BMW factory supported no fewer than nine satellite 'works' teams, some being as far-flung as in Australia and South Africa. Manufacturers' and drivers' championships were won consistently and in profusion until the regulations were gradually altered, to give a considerable (up to 110lb/50kg) minimum-weight advantage to front-wheel-drive cars.

When it became clear that 3-Series cars would no longer be allowed to compete on equal terms with their front-wheel-drive rivals, BMW withdrew its cars from Touring Car racing. For the year 2000 and beyond, in any case, it proposed to spend its motorsport budgets on new V10 F1 engines, which were to be fitted exclusively to the cars of the Williams team.

Even so, in 1998, BMW 3-Series cars won race victories in 11 countries, and took 21 championship titles. By the end of the year, 3-Series cars had won no fewer than 29 International Championships since 1993.

Incidentally, 1998 was the year when a specially-developed E46 320d became the first-ever diesel-engined car to win a long-distance international endurance event – the 24-hour race at the Nurburgring, in Germany.

They might not have been M3s, but they looked like M3s and were even faster! In Europe in the early 1990s, Touring Car race regulations were written to impose 2-litre engines, so BMW chose to use further-developed versions of the old-style four-cylinder M3 engine. Until two-door cars were banned (decisions, decisions . . .), BMW race cars were actually re-engined 318iS types looking rather like specially liveried M3s, which did wonders for their image.

customers a year, many of them in the USA, could not possibly be wrong . . .

BMW, in any case, handed them a sop in 1994 by introducing a very limited-production M3 GT, a much-modified version of the E36 Coupe, complete with 295bhp engine, front airdam 'splitter', two-tier rear spoiler, and many interior trim items made from Kevlar. Only 396 such cars were built, all with left-hand drive and all for sale in Europe (but not the UK).

For the American market, too, at the same time the M3 Lightweight (coupe) became available, still with the same 243bhp engine, but with no sunroof, no insulation, no radio equipment and no air-conditioning, but with aluminium doors and a rear spoiler. All this was a mild attempt to provide a car which could be raced – and it flopped, for only about 85 such cars were produced.

M3 Evolution
Less than three years after the E36 had been introduced, and little more than a year after the four-door saloon version had gone on sale, BMW then took the six-cylinder M3 concept a full stage further,

and it was that legendary character Paul Rosche (with his Motorsport work) who should take much of the credit. The original type was discontinued, and all three versions were replaced by a further-developed version, officially called (though not badged) the M3 Evolution.

As expected of BMW, this was not just an excuse to dabble, or just to produce a more powerful engine, but an exercise to rework the chassis in many other respects. The problem for the enthusiast was how to begin to describe the latest machine, for if the original six-cylinder M3s were 'supercars', what on earth were they to call the late-1995 variety? Visually there were almost no changes – unless you looked at spoilers and grilles – but here was another silky-smooth car which was more powerful, better-equipped, even more completely developed and still totally flexible. Yet if this was a pussy-cat, it had even bigger claws . . .

This time, in fact, BMW concentrated its efforts on the running gear – on the engine and the transmission. Somehow the engine had been stretched even further – to 3,201cc – and henceforth it would have not

The M Coupe, a combination of the Z3 structure, the M3 engine and a new type of hatchback styling, went on sale in 1997. Aesthetics? Make up your own mind . . .

single, but double VANOS control (which therefore worked on *both* camshafts), and hid much of the unique-to-McLaren BMW V12 component detail inside, while using the most recently developed MSS50 engine management system. The McLaren's V12, incidentally, had a bore and stroke of 86 x 87mm, whereas the M3 Evo unit measured

---

New management system provides more power and efficiency

86.4 x 91mm – not the same, but obviously closely related. Remembering that this family of straight-six engines had started out as a unit measuring 80 x

66mm/1,990cc in 1977, one marvels at how the 'stretch' had been achieved.

Yet here was an engine which was still smooth, torquey, flexible and fuel-efficient, and there was even more innovation in the Evolution model. Not only did the new 3.2-litre engine produce 321bhp at 7,400rpm, but a new BMW/Siemens-developed management system made for even more efficient engine management, made the exhaust 'cleaner' than ever before, yet the car could still run on normal grades of unleaded fuel, and could meet every known exhaust and noise pollution regulation in the world.

The latest double VANOS variable valve timing helped bring the torque peak down by 350rpm and made the engine even more flexible in meeting every demand. Unique to the M3 at this stage, it would of course be applied to the new-generation E46 328i in 1998.

To match the brawnier engine, BMW also provided a new six-speed transmission (where sixth was an 'overdrive'), which had

The M3's six-cylinder, 3.2-litre Evolution engine was carefully packaged, with unique manifolding and different installation details. This, in fact, was the engine bay of the Z3-based M Roadster, but the M3 engine bay looked much the same.

evolved from that used in the contemporary M5. This, allied to a lower (shorter) final drive ratio of 3.23:1, gave the M3 Evolution even better acceleration with improved fuel consumption. Thus equipped, the electronically-limited 155mph/250kph top speed was available in sixth *and* fifth gears, which meant than on limit-free roads the latest M3 was at least the equal of anything except the most determinedly driven Porsches or Ferraris.

The Americans, unfortunately, were only offered a 3,152cc, 243bhp version of this car, with a five-speed transmission. But in view of the very tight speed limits which have always applied in the USA – even Montana, once limit-free, came back into line with a 75mph limit in 1999 – this was still no real hardship. If you ever meet a North American who asks you what all the M3 fuss is about, try to arrange for him to have a demonstration in the 321bhp version – whose power/weight ratio is 32 per cent higher than the one he usually drives . . .

To match the new engine, its colossal acceleration, and the sheer Teutonic efficiency of it all, BMW had also reworked the suspension yet again. The rear track was actually slightly narrower than before – this having been done to incorporate wider rear tyres inside the existing sheet-metal bodywork – 850i-type front wheel mountings had been added, and there were stiffened-up springs, anti-roll bars and damper settings.

The sensitive power-assisted steering had been re-valved, to feel 6 per cent 'quicker' than before, the brakes had been enlarged and upgraded by using M5 components (the fronts now using the floating disc principle), and the latest type of Teves IV ABS control had been added.

Now, too, there were different wheels and tyres at both front and rear – 225/45-17 tyres on 7.5-inch front rims, 245/40-17 tyres on 8.5-inch rear rims – which balanced the high-speed handling even better than before, and ensured rear-drive traction in all but the most unfavourable conditions. The new car was also lightened as far as possible by having aluminium doors, which saved 44lb/20kg. Although it was still a visually understated car (no rear spoiler, no wheelarch extensions and no additional bonnet louvres, of course), it was an impressively developed and superb high-performance package which looked, felt and performed like lightning.

In its first full year, 1996, no fewer than 11,789 M3s were delivered, of which 6,896 were Coupes, 3,639 were saloons and 1,254 were Cabriolets. British prices started at £36,550, which made some of their domestic competition look a bit sick.

All this, however, was just another junction in a still-evolving story. Against all expectations, BMW then announced that they would make automatic transmission optional on M3s – slipping this change rather casually into the options list in 1996, though it was not for sale in every market, notably not in the UK: this was the same ZF five-speeder which was already optional in other 3-Series models.

In mid-1996, too (but not actually available as an option until 1997), a new type of six-speed transmission was also revealed for the M3, this being titled the Sequential M Gearbox (SMG). In many ways this was a perfect halfway house between manual and automatic transmission, for it successfully provided clutchless gearchanges, which were allied to the same six-speed manual transmission as before.

The conventional clutch pedal had been completely eliminated, for there was an automatic, hydraulically controlled take-up from rest (and automatic disengagement when coming to rest) and to look after normal gearchanging, this all being operated from a robust push/pull centrally-mounted lever which also matched the change to what it sensed as the driver's habits. Like the more conventional BMW Steptronic automatic transmission (which I specified for my own 1999 E46 328i), it gave a very Touring Car racer type of feel to the change – where all upward changes meant banging the lever straight forward against a stop (after which it sprang back to a central position), and all downward changes meant pulling it backwards.

To quote *Autocar* : 'The concept alone is enough to have most enthusiasts drooling in anticipation . . . it is the very embodiment of touring car technology meets luxury saloon.'

By the end of 1997, therefore, the E36 M3 concept had developed into a complete range, with a choice of three body styles and three transmissions, plus a host of extremely desirable extras to boost the specification even further. In spite of the high prices, this was value-for-money 'supercar motoring' with a vengeance, and it explains why there was never any let-up in demand.

However, as the range of new mainstream E46 3-Series cars built up in 1998 and 1999 (saloons first, Coupes next and Tourings from mid-1999), it was clear that more innovation and a new-style E46 M3 was already on the way. The last of the E36-style M3 saloons was built in the winter of 1997/98, and the final E36-type M3 Coupes and Cabriolets left the factory in the winter of 1998/99.

Yet there was no immediate replacement for these cars. BMW, it seemed, was too busy with finalizing the new-generation (and larger) M5, and the launch of a new-generation M3 was to be delayed until 2000, although the first official pictures of the 3.4-litre engined car were shown in September 1999. Nevertheless the wait would not be wasted.

M Roadster
Although this car will be described in more detail in Chapter 7, I should also note here the arrival of the first-ever open two-seater M-Series BMW – the M Roadster of 1997. By this time, BMW had started building cars in the USA (at Spartanburg, South Carolina), one of the new models to be produced there being a two-seater sports car, the Z3, which was based on the Compact platform and chassis.

For sale in Europe, the M-Roadster came complete with the latest 321bhp/3.2-litre engine, but only a five-speed gearbox, this being the very first M-Series BMW to be assembled in the USA. It was yet another indication of BMW's future global ambitions.

CHAPTER 5

CABRIOLETS AND TOURINGS

Sharing the E36 style

Although new drop-top and load-carrying versions of the E36 3-Series were always planned – and in 1991 BMW made no attempt to hide what was to come – they did not appear until 1993 and 1994.

In the interim, BMW carried on making old-style Cabriolets and Tourings in larger numbers, which meant that there were two distinctly different generations of 3-Series in the showrooms for a full four years.

The same situation would apply, too, at the end of the 1990s, for the cars I am about to describe were still being made and sold for more than two years after the fourth-generation E46 saloons and Coupes had already gone on sale. Nothing new here, or anything unique either, for other companies did – and still do – the same thing.

Open-air 3-Series
As far as the 3-Series BMW was concerned, Cabriolets had a lengthy pedigree. The original soft-top 3-Series cars had been bodied by Baur, of Stuttgart, from 1977, though BMW later developed and launched its own-design E30 drop-top in 1985. With a two-door style and full four-seater accommodation, clearly this was a template for what was to follow.

After the new E36 cars were put on sale in 1991, however, seasons came and went, the old-style E30 Cabriolet stayed on the market, and there were persistent rumours that to develop a new-generation model was all too much trouble.

Not so. Behind the scenes in Munich, the engineering team had been beavering away for years, not only trying to develop a typically smooth, draught-free and versatile new model, but one that would not carry the same substantial weight penalty as before. When the E30 Cabriolet had been launched in 1985, BMW admitted that, like for like, cutting off the roof and reinforcing the underside to beef up the stiffness of the remaining structure had involved a penalty of no less than 290lb/131kg – the equivalent of carrying

---

Paring weight in a Cabriolet is no simple matter

---

two 10-stone adults in the car at all times.

In the end, as the statistics show, they were only a little bit more successful in paring weight in the new model. When launched at the end of 1992, engine for engine, the new Cabriolet was officially stated to weigh 265lb/120kg more than the equivalent saloon. In spite of cutting off the roof and providing only two doors, the platform (and its unseen underpinnings)

Although the new Cabriolet, which was unveiled in 1993, had much new engineering in its two-door bodyshell, it was all based on the same advanced platform and running gear as the modern E36 saloons and Coupes. This 'ghosted' study emphasizes the bulk of the complex rear suspension.

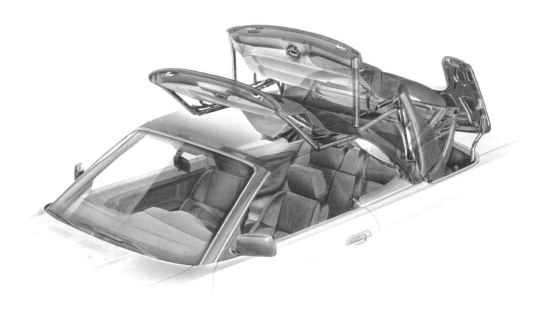

Not only was the fold-down soft-top of the new Cabriolet as carefully engineered as the rest of the car, but when not in use it stowed away under a pivotting metal cover behind the rear seats.

Following the success of the earlier-generation Touring models, it was inevitable that there would be a new-generation Touring in the mid-1990s. Then, and now, however, BMW refused to allow the words 'estate car' to be used to describe this machine!

Although we must call this car a Touring, to keep BMW happy, in every other motoring observer's language it is an estate car, complete with substantial loading space, a split rear seat backrest and a fold-down facility.

still needed a considerable amount of beefing-up.

Styled, engineered and built 'in house', the new Cabriolet was, in many ways, closer to the E36 Coupe than to the saloon. All these cars shared the same basic pressed-steel platform, of course, but the Cabriolet had the same windscreen shape and profile as the Coupe (which, as pointed out in Chapter 3, was raked further than that of the saloon), and used the same longer door shells. The screen surround, of course, was considerably beefed-up to provide a degree of roll-over protection. Aft of the doors, and below the waistline, the new Cabriolet shared much the same profile and detailing as the Coupe.

Stiffening-up the roofless shell to pass the latest, and very stringent, crash test regulations had involved adding extra box members under the floor, along with stiffening-up the sills, bulkhead and the structure behind the passenger seats. Typically, BMW made sure that this was nowhere obvious from outside the car, though a worm's-eye view of the shell would have pointed up the additional members.

As with the previous 3-Series Cabriolet, the soft-top was a big and carefully engineered assembly. Lower-priced versions (for this car would eventually be available with all the petrol engines in the 3-Series range, though never with diesels) had a manually-operated hood, but an electrically-powered version was always optional, or even standard equipment on the most upmarket versions.

Nor was it merely an electric option developed and provided in isolation, for a truly ingenious package had been provided. After pressing one button, all four side windows (door and rear-quarter glass, that is) dropped flush into the door caps, then after pressing the next button the roof could lift up from the screen rail and fold away under a flush-fitting canopy behind the rear seats. The only DIY work needed was to latch, or unlatch a single fixing on the screen rail itself.

All this, of course, was allied to a roll-over bar which remained flat, and invisible, behind the rear seats until sensors detected a roll, when it sprung up in what seemed like no time at all. Optional, too, was a wind deflector, which could be fitted above and behind the rear seats, along with all the goodies already listed for Coupes and saloons – including M-Technic sports suspension and those excellent front sports seats.

In fairness, however, this was no more nor less than one might expect of such a car – though it was still a real, as opposed to an idealized, offering and it still wasn't perfect. At lower speeds there could be quite a lot of scuttle shake and general fidgeting around over uneven surfaces, while the boot was unavoidably smaller than that of the Coupe, though still reasonably adequate.

Although it was originally sold only with

New in 1985, this was the previous-series Cabriolet, which proved a great success, on which the new E36-variety 3-Series Cabriolet set out to improve.

the 192bhp/2.5-litre 24-valve 'six', within three years the Cabriolet line-up had been fully developed, with a wide range of engine options starting from the 115bhp/1.8-litre eight-valve 'four', and moving up through the 150bhp/2.0-litre 24-valve 'six', and on through the 2.5-litre 'six' even to (from 1995) the alloy-blocked 193bhp/2.8-litre 24-valve 'six'. Even though the Cabriolet was neither as aerodynamically smooth, nor as light as

the saloon, the 328i-engined version was capable of 137mph/220kph. A 316i Cabriolet was never made available, for this version would have been unacceptably slow by BMW standards.

Sensibly, though, BMW never offered this car with any of the diesel engines, though they had such confidence in the structure that they also offered it in M3 form, the most powerful of which produced 321bhp, as I have already

Except for the detail around the screen rail and the switchgear provided to operate the electric folding mechanism, the Cabriolet's facia/instrument display was just like that of other E36-family 3-Series cars.

Announced in 1993, the new-style 3-Series Cabriolet was clearly a close relative of the saloon and Coupe types, sharing the same basic doors as the Coupe. From the nose to the front bulkhead/windscreen, the sheet metal, packaging and engine installations were common between all types. Note that the wheels on this particular car were optional extras.

The mid-1990s 3-Series Cabriolet is an extremely elegant and versatile car, significantly more expensive than the steel-top saloons, but in some ways even more satisfying. Hood down and (optional) air-conditioning in action, this is a pleasant way of enjoying the summer in any country. Once again, this car is equipped with one of BMW's range of optional wheels.

BMW's assembly plants – Germany and Austria

It is many years since all BMW assembly was confined to the parent factory in Munich, though at the end of the century this continued to be the major source of four-door 3-Series saloons and three-door Compacts, 180,000 cars being built there every year. From the mid-1960s, steady expansion caused BMW to look for alternative centres of supply.

Another small Bavarian enterprise, Hans Glas, was purchased in 1966, whose factory at Dingolfing (an hour's drive to the north-east of Munich) has subsequently been expanded enormously. By the end of the 1990s, Dingolfing concentrated on building all non-3-Series models, but there was still space for some 3-Series saloons to pour out of the plant as well. Dingolfing was a latecomer to the 3-Series programme, using a night shift to find the capacity, with complete bodyshells being supplied from Regensburg.

By the end of the 1990s, the Regensburg plant (due north of Munich, about an hour out of town and just 20 miles from Dingolfing) was concentrating on building 3-Series models, mainly Tourings, Cabriolets and Coupes, though once again there was some capacity for 3-Series saloons also to be erected. In 1998, the first full year of E46 assembly, 182,000 cars were produced.

The largest and most important manufacturing factory outside Germany was the Steyr plant in Austria, which was close to Linz, and perhaps three hours by truck from any of the car assembly complexes. By the end of the century, nearly 500,000 engines of all types were being produced every year.

Especially on larger cars, it is difficult to provide good lines for a Cabriolet when the soft-top is furled – yet BMW managed it. The soft-top is tucked away under the hinged metal panel behind the rear seats, with only limited impact on luggage space.

The new-generation E36 Touring was not introduced until 1994, being the fourth derivative of the E36 platform which had begun its career in 1991. More rounded, where the previous model had been a little angular, the latest five-door Touring became a great success – though its relatively short career was never expected to survive the end of the Century!

This BMW (GB) publicity shot carefully poses an upmarket Cabriolet (complete with optional wheels) in the suitably sybaritic atmosphere of a race course.

recorded in Chapter 4.

Even after the new-shape E46 saloon had appeared, the existing Cabriolet continued to sell strongly, no fewer than 27,900 examples being assembled in 1998. BMW, however, was in no hurry to replace the existing model, and even though 'sneak' pictures of a new-generation model appeared in the autumn of 1999, sales were not scheduled to begin until 2000.

What's in a name?

For many years, neither BMW nor its main German rival, Mercedes-Benz, was prepared to market an estate car. BMW had once produced a 2000 Touring, but that was a three-door hatchback, had not been a commercial success, and didn't really count. For many years, I am convinced, both companies thought that load-carrying cars were below the dignity of their perceived images. They also thought that if they stubbornly ignored the requests which were building up in their dealers' showrooms, these would simply go away.

But far from going away, they grew in intensity, and it was Volvo's success in this market sector which eventually tipped the balance. It was Mercedes-Benz who succumbed first, in 1978, which must have made life a little difficult for BMW, though they still held out until late 1987, when a five-door version of the E30 design called the Touring was introduced.

Although all physical and visual evidence was to the contrary, BMW insisted that the Touring was not – repeat *not* – an estate car, and as BMW's British concessionaire boss Paul Layzell commented at the time: 'The word "estate" is banned here. We see the car as appealing to the sporting driver who needs a little extra room, to accommodate a growing family, for example. It was not designed as a load-carrier in the Volvo estate sense . . .'

Fine words – *brave* words even – but in spite of their wide-eyed innocence, BMW had no chance of convincing press and customers about that philosophy. The Touring, after all, not only had a full five-door estate car style, a lift-up tailgate whose lip extended down to the 'loading' (sorry about that) platform, but it also had fold-down rear seats which could make

This was the previous, and original, 3-Series Touring (of 1987 to 1994), which had been a limited success, but by providing better packaging BMW thought they could offer more. On the older car, in particular, the tail-lamp clusters got in the way of loading bulky objects.

that 'loading' platform extend still further.

Because the E30 Touring did not actually go on sale until the winter of 1987/88, it only had a relatively short career. Although it was one of the 'hang-over' models which remained in production after the first of the new-generation E36 types had arrived in 1990/91, it was finally dropped in 1994. Its replacement was the smooth, subtly styled and still estate car-like and highly versatile E36 Touring.

It seems that the arrival of the new-generation Touring, in fairness, had been delayed at the request of BMW's number-crunchers, the accountants, so that the *old* type of Touring could go on as long as possible and so wring the most out of its specialized production tooling. Maybe they were right – because ultimately 105,000 examples were sold!

There seems to be no doubt that the new E36 Touring might have appeared much earlier than it did – and the fact that the fourth-generation E46 Touring appeared in 1999 meant that it would be on the market for less than five years.

Once again, BMW wanted to position its five-door model away from other, rival, manufacturers. Months before it officially went on sale, company spokesmen insisted that this was a 'lifestyle-orientated car that puts more emphasis on driver appeal than outright load-carrying ability . . . The Touring is positioned differently. It will give added practicality without sacrificing performance and driver enjoyment . . .' But, to bowdlerise another famous remark from earlier times: 'Well, they would say that, wouldn't they?'.

The first official pictures of the E36 Touring were released in November 1994, though there was little technical detail, and it was pointed out that the first deliveries would not take place until the first weeks of 1995. This was the moment when BMW merely pointed out the smoother styling (so closely based on that of the four-door saloon, though with different rear-seat doors), the more capacious and wider interior and the fact that the rear hatch was somewhat larger. [All the more convenient, therefore, to instal those non-existent bulky loads that BMW would rather not talk about!]

This was the profile of the E36 Touring, introduced in 1994 and built until 1999, when it was replaced by the new-generation E46 variety. For an engineer, it is always fascinating to spot how and where another bodyshell has been altered – for this car shared the E36 saloon's platform, nose, windscreen and front doors – but the rest of the shell was unique. The only thing missing – and BMW insisted that there was little demand for it – was a four-wheel-drive version!

The 'office' of the E36 Touring made no concessions to the fact that this was a load-carrier as well as a fast car, for it was as fully equipped as expected. Cars of this type had optional ZF five-speed automatic transmission, complete with a semi-manual selection feature, plus Sport, Economy and Winter modes.

This was the load area in the tail of the E36 Touring, showing the way that luggage or stowed kit could be hidden away under the pull-out cover, and the way that the rear seats could be split and folded down, separately or together. Just like an estate car really – but don't let BMW hear you using that phrase!

BMW, in fact, had good cause to be proud of the style, and the packaging. From the nose to the rear of the front doors, this was really the same car as the four-door saloon, but from that plane aft, it was all new. The waistline seemed to go on rising, gently, to the tail-lamps, the rear doors were certainly larger (with much more glass area than those of the saloon), and the Touring's 'greenhouse' was at once rounded but spacious, nicely detailed, and had a built-in wiper/washer which pivoted at waist level.

This car was, in fact, exactly the same length as the saloon, which meant that the saloon's regrettably small boot had been translated into a regrettably small loading space in the Touring. On this car the problem was that the ingenious new Z-axle rear suspension didn't allow the load floor to be dropped any further, and the sizeable wheelarches endemic in the same layout also rather narrowed the width.

Yet none of this mattered, or was seen to matter, for the new Touring handled and performed like a sports saloon, was so well-built that it felt rock-solid, and seemed to suffer from no drawbacks, not even heavier fuel consumption. All the usual kit and the choice of optional extra 'toys' were available, there was a full range of engines and transmissions and, yes, maybe this was exactly the sort of machine one needed to stow the mountain bikes, the hang-glider and the other leisure-time accessories in the tail. As you might expect, a discreet but removable loading bay cover was standard, as were anchors in the loading deck for lashing down all the gear.

Was BMW's 'lifestyle' character paint-job accurate? Perhaps *Autocar*'s testers can tell us most in their summary of the new 328i Touring:

'The five-door, rear-drive, straight-six formula is traditional to a fault. But the attractive shape, flattering and entertaining drive line and one of the finest sixes in existence take the conventions of the small estate car and re-establish them on a higher plane. Because of this, people will flock to it, and we don't blame them. But if your car must be estate first and performance car second, the 328i Touring is not for you.'

Clearly, though, it was right for many, many people, for in a five-year life, 130,000 were sold. At its peak, in 1997/98, the Touring was available in 316i, 318i, 320i, 323i, 328i, 318tds and 325tds types, with a spread of power from 90bhp (318tds) to 193bhp (328i). Yet again this was a successful 3-Series enterprise, which BMW then supplanted with a new type of Touring in the autumn of 1999.

The 316i Compact was indeed the 'entry level' machine in BMW's mid-1990s range of cars, for not only was it the smallest in the entire line-up, but also the cheapest of all 3-Series types. Even so, a 316i could reach 117mph, and beat 10 seconds in the 0-60mph traffic-light sprint.

CHAPTER 6

COMPACT

BMW's first hatchback

Rumours of a smaller, hatchback version of the E36 3-Series began to circulate in the spring of 1993, but the new derivative, badged 'Compact', was not officially previewed until the end of the year, with sales starting in the first weeks of 1994.

Here was an interesting concept, and a fascinating way of expanding the entire 3-Series range. The two-door style, complete with a large hatchback, was altogether more stubby than before, while aft of the front seats, the platform, rear suspension and structure were all different.

At first glance, BMW enthusiasts were somewhat alarmed by what the new-style Compact represented, for here was a practical hatchback rather than a sporting and executive saloon, not at all what the traditionalists would expect from BMW. Worse – according to them, though perhaps they had not thought through the marketing stance being taken up – this car was only to be sold with some of the lower-powered engines, and was meant to be for utility purposes and the family man, rather than for the executive or the sportsman.

Wild rumours that BMW were trying to match VW's Golf were wide of the mark, though stories that they were aiming to recapture previous BMW '02' users were more accurate. Although scoop pictures showed a car quite obviously based on the E36 3-Series layout, but with a shortened tail which incorporated a full-depth tailgate/hatchback, it was not until full details were handed out that one realized the extent of the re-engineering that had been needed.

It was the repackaging of the rear end which had caused a wholesale redesign (and even, though it was never admitted, the eating of so many pious words . . .). Although the 106.3in/2,700mm wheelbase dimension of the four-door car was retained, under the skin the middle part and rear end of the platform was entirely new, not only somewhat shorter behind the rear wheels, but with a reversion to old-style semi-trailing arm independent rear suspension.

Although BMW had officially ditched this type when launching the new E36 a few years earlier, it now acknowledged that the new-type multi-link suspension was bulky and took up too much space. Accordingly, for E36/5 (as the Compact was coded) the old-style suspension, complete with its known deficiences in terms of tyre grip and camber change under load, came back.

This, BMW claimed, allowed the boot/loading floor to be lowered by several inches (very important when load-carrying was considered), and allowed for the rear seats to fold down in the best hatchback manner. The fuel tank was still positioned under the rear seat, but it had had to be reshaped and reduced to 52 litres (from 65 litres), and instead of a full-size spare wheel and tyre, a small 'space-saver' spare wheel was provided.

In all other respects, which included retention of the entire E36 front end,

Under the skin, the Compact was different in many ways from the E36 four-door saloon, for aft of the front seats the platform was completely different, as was the structure, which had to accommodate completely different rear suspension and a hatchback feature.

From this angle, side-on, the Compact's rather truncated tail is obvious. BMW had set out to produce an 'entry-level' 3-Series, not only with rather simplified equipment, but with a shorter tail and a lift-up hatchback. To make sure that there was enough stowage space inside the tailgate, the old type of semi-trailing link rear suspension had to be specified.

Open wide! Compared with the four-door saloon, the Compact retained the standard wheelbase, but had a much reduced overhang behind the rear wheels. A full-depth lift-up hatchback was standard, this being an interesting combination of Coupe (two-door), and Touring (load-carrier). The type of wheels on this particular car were optional extras.

When the Compact range was introduced, the 318ti version had a 140bhp/1,796cc four-cylinder, twin-cam engine – which was enough to give it a 128mph top speed. All this for £15,290 (plus the cost of extras like the Sports Pack, including five-spoke alloys on this particular car) ensured a ready sale.

suspension and steering, a disc/drum braking set-up on the 316i version (with ABS as standard), and a choice of five-speed manual or four-speed automatic transmissions, the first wave of Compacts was as expected.

At first the only available model was the 316i Compact, whose engine was the familiar single-cam/eight-valve, 102bhp/1,596cc 'four' which had a truly venerable history, though within months the more upmarket 318ti Compact joined in, complete with the latest twin-cam/16-valve, 140bhp/1,796cc version of the same power unit, and four-wheel disc brakes.

From the rear, the hatchback feature, combined with an overall length shorter by 8.8in/223mm, gave the new car rather a stunted aspect, though from the front end there was no way of picking three-door from four-door types, as the same front end sheet metal and styling was used. This also showed up in the aerodynamic performance, for the Cd slipped from 0.29 (saloon) to 0.33 (Compact). Compared with the four-door saloon, more structural weight had been needed around the rear end, so there was a like-for-like 110lb/50kg weight penalty.

The facia/instrument display was new, and somewhat simplified, the front seats of course were arranged to fold forward to give easy access to the rear seats, while there was a 50/50 per cent split of the rear seat squab to make the Compact a versatile and competitive load carrier.

Even though this was bound to be a controversial car, for a trade-off of rear suspension behaviour had to be made against better rear-end packaging and convenience, BMW made it clear that for the rest of the 1990s at least this would be the smallest – and cheapest – BMW they would make. Customers, it was suggested, should judge the Compact on that basis, rather than as a stripped-out and simplified version of the saloons.

Independent road tests soon confirmed that the Compact was still gratifyingly brisk (even the 102bhp car could reach 117mph in fifth gear), and that the latest version of semi-trailing link rear suspension was still surprisingly capable, with a class-competitive ride; also praised were the good brakes and satisfactory level of equipment.

None of this, however, would count for much unless the price was right – and it was. When the 316i Compact went on sale in Britain in October 1994, it cost £13,650 at a time when the equivalent 316i four-door saloon was priced at £15,225 and the new 316i Coupe was listed at £16,460. No-one– absolutely no-one – complained about that!

Nor, it seemed, did anyone elsewhere in BMW's world. Even before the end of 1994, 63,810 Compacts had been manufactured, 69,484 more followed in 1995, after which demand settled down to around 60,000 every year.

More derivatives

During the next two years or so, the range of Compacts was built up in the same

For the Compact model, BMW provided a facia/instrument display which was much different from that of the saloons, Coupes and Cabriolets – in fact with much in common with the forthcoming Z3 sports car. The steering wheel, in particular, looked more bulky and not as delicate.

logical process as was being applied to the saloons, first with the arrival of a more powerful petrol engine, and then with the addition of a 90bhp four-cylinder turbodiesel. At every stage, it seemed, BMW wanted to gain from the 'economies of scale', by making all its 3-Series cars as commonized as possible.

For the 318ti Compact, therefore, the engine was the familiar 16-valve/140bhp 'four' of 1,796cc, as already found in the 318iS Coupe types, this being matched to a chassis incorporating four-wheel disc brakes, higher overall gearing and wider-section tyres.

This was a very appealing package (which, in Britain, cost just £1,940 more than the entry-level 316i Compact), and if BMW had not already won so many hearts with other 140bhp-engined versions of the same car, it might have gained an even higher reputation. For the moment, forget the other 3-Series derivatives, and ask yourselves whether a 128mph maximum speed, 0-60mph acceleration in less than 10 seconds and overall fuel consumption of up to 30mpg was not very attractive?

As in the other 3-Series models, the 90bhp/1,665cc diesel engine was a great disappointment, for although it might have been very economical, its performance was very disappointing. As diesel fuel was by no means as cheap as in other markets, it was no coincidence that this model made little impact on the British market – or that a number of customers made sure that the badge was left off the tailgate!

That, you might have thought, was all the Compact range which BMW needed, but their original intention – to fit only four-cylinder engines up front – was soon to be abandoned. In 1994, top brass had said there were no plans to fit six-cylinder engines into these cars, though at the same time they agreed that it would be a straightforward enough task to do so. The packaging and layout of the front end, after all, was the same as that of other 3-Series types. [Conversion specialists soon proved that this was, indeed, the case, with at least one monstrously powerful M3 version being produced!]

But such resolution was soon abandoned, and the 323ti eventually made its bow before the end of 1997. With 170bhp of silky 2.5-litre power, here was a stirring engine to give *real* performance to the three-door model. Visually, of course, there were a few changes, including different front, side and rear skirts, but otherwise one could only pick out the six-cylinder-engined model by the type of wheels fitted. To lift the bonnet and peer into the engine bay was merely to confirm that the front end was almost identical to the latest 323i saloons and Coupes.

The good news was that such a fast car had been announced, but the bad news was that it was not to be sold in every market, the British one in particular. The reason for this was one of marketing rather than engineering, for since BMW only planned to build around 2,000 323ti Compacts in a year, they were not willing to make a small number of those in right-hand-drive form – especially as they would be direct competitors to the latest 323i Coupe, which cost more and was very profitable!

3-Series popularity

Snobs may still call the 3-Series an exclusive car for the rich (how wrong can they be?), but a snapshot of production in a single year shows the depth of demand for the cars.

In 1998 alone, BMW built no less than 429,900 of what management called their 'small-car series' – a total which included 146,250 four-door E46 saloons, about 60,000 of the E36-family Compacts, 27,900 Cabriolets and 28,100 Tourings, the balance being E36 or E46-type Coupes and Z3 Roadster/Coupes, more than 160,000 in all.

Compared with simultaneous annual figures of 221,600 5-Series and 47,200 7-Series models, this was a truly remarkable achievement.

So, where did these cars sell? In Germany alone, BMW delivered a total of 232,500 cars of all types, in the USA 131,600, and in the UK no fewer than 64,200 – in each case 3-Series cars accounting for more than half of the total numbers.

From June 1999 BMW offered an 'Open Air' version of the Compact, complete with a full-length fold-back sunroof. Because of the short length of the roof panel, there has never been enough space for the conventional slide-back steel item.

Such frustrated markets missed a well-equipped and desirable machine which had not only been re-engined, but reworked to suit. The engine was backed by even higher overall gearing than before, with a five-speed manual or a *five*-speed automatic transmission (the only five-speeder in this sub-range), the suspension had been tightened-up, the ride height was lower by 0.6in/15mm, tyre sizes had crept up to 225/50-16in, there was a revised interior which included sports front seats, while a trip computer, central locking and electric window lifts were all standard.

Performance? A rousing 143mph top speed, 0-60mph in only 7.5 seconds, and typical mid-range response for which this six-cylinder engine was already famous, produced the sort of 3-Series BMW which had to give best only to the mighty M3.

Even after the new E46-style saloons were introduced early in 1998, production of the original Compact series continued, full blast, at Munich, with 60,000 being built that year, and there seemed to be no

diminution of their appeal. Although BMW readily admitted that, one day, a second-generation E46-based Compact would appear, there seemed to be no rush to bring it forward, for it was not even scheduled for preview until the year 2000. By this time, it was clear, more than 400,000 of the original type would have been built – no gamble after all, but a highly profitable project.

Z3 – a Roadster derivative

The development and arrival of BMW's two-seater Z3 Roadster is charted in the next Chapter, so at this point I only need to point out that without the Compact, in economic and investment terms, the Z3 could never have been designed. Simply, and basically, the Z3 – even the rip-roaring 321bhp M-Roadster derivative of it – was designed around the Compact's version of the E36 platform and the old-style semi-trailing link independent rear suspension. There were, of course, many other technical links (*see Chapter 7 for details*).

CHAPTER 7

BLOOD RELATIONS

Z3 and 5-Series

It would be a big mistake to consider the development of 3-Series cars on their own, for they have always been a part – a very important part – of BMW's overall range. Although, at any one time, the 3-Series has always been BMW's best-selling range, these cars have always run in harness with larger cars like the 5-Series and 7-Series models, and with specialized types like the 6-Series and 8-Series Coupes – not only in style, but in engineering philosophy and in the sharing of components.

In the 1980s and 1990s, two cars, in particular, always had technical links and (sometimes) shared components with the 3-Series – these being the Z3 Roadster and the 5-Series range. This made a lot of commercial sense, but for owners of all types it was also reassuring.

Z3: the 'James Bond' BMW

In the 1970s and 1980s BMW would have nothing to do with the open 'Roadster' market, concentrating instead on dramatically fast saloons and coupes such as the M3, the M5 and the M635CSi. Then, in the 1990s, the company lifted its horizons and elected to expand into USA-based manufacture.

The first rumours of a new 'small' sports

Z3, the very first USA-built BMW, was a clever amalgam of 3-Series engineering and equipment, built up on a Compact platform, with unique two-seater styling.

car from BMW began to circulate in 1992, and by August of 1993 BMW confirmed that, when ready, this model would be built at a new green-field factory in the USA. At that stage, the pundits knew nothing, but could only guess that it would somehow have to be related to the new E36 3-Series family.

The published guesses were only partially accurate. *Autocar & Motor* forecast at this time that: 'BMW has decided to retain a substantial section of the old 3-Series platform, including the rear suspension, rather than adopt the more complex set-up of the current [E36] range . . .'

They and other more excitable 'what-if' forecasters, however, had already picked up a new codename – Z21 – and the fact that open two-seater and coupe derivatives, plus the use of 'fours' and 'sixes', were already being planned.

By mid-1994, BMW's new factory at Spartanburg, South Carolina, was almost complete, but there was no official news about the new Z3 Roadster until mid-1995. By then, the news had already broken that prototype Z3s were to be used in the latest James Bond film, *Goldeneye* – which didn't go down very well with British patriots, who thought that 'James Bond' should always use a British car!

Even then, full technical details of the car were held back until November 1995, and first deliveries (initially to the USA market) did not begin until the winter of 1995/96. It was only then that the Z3's close relationship, and technical links, with the 3-Series Compact (not the 3-Series saloons or Coupes) became apparent, for the technical data rapidly made it clear that the monocoque Z3 structure was being built up around a Compact platform, and its old-style (E30-type) semi-trailing link independent rear suspension.

But not exactly the same platform, as this table makes clear:

Model	Z3 Roadster	3-Series Compact
Wheelbase (in)	96.3	106.3
Front track (in)	55.9	55.9
Rear track (in)	56.1	56.1
Overall length (in)	158.4	165.7
Unladen weight (lb)	2,585	2,646
1.9-litre engine	140bhp/ 1,895cc	140bhp/ 1,895cc

The truly important difference was that because the Z3 was meant to be no more than a comfortable two-seater, the wheelbase had been shortened by a full 10 inches, and the overall length by 7.3

Although only evolutionary in concept compared with the previous 5-Series, the 5-Series car introduced in 1995 still had many features which were familiar in the E36 3-Series, notably the lift-up door handles, the over-hanging boot style and the compact rear-lamp clusters.

In some ways, the Z1 roadster, which sold in limited numbers in the late 1980s, was the spiritual predecessor to the Z3 and the 3-Series saloons; to the Z3 because of its two-seater layout, and to the E36 3-Series because of the way it pioneered the multi-link rear suspension. On the Z1, incidentally, the doors did not open outwards, but retracted downwards into the sturdy sills.

For BMW the Z3 was a pioneering car in so many ways – the first two-seater to be developed from a saloon platform, the first BMW sports car to be built in the USA, and the first to star in a 'James Bond' film! Original types only had four-cylinder engines.

inches, that difference in reduction being explained by the very stubby rear end of the Roadster. Engineers looking up from underneath the car would see that the steel structure, the layout of the pressings and the stress paths of the underside were nearly identical, all the way from the nose back to a position immediately under/behind the front seats, after which the Compact floorpan had clearly been truncated and its rear suspension brought considerably closer to the line of those seats.

BMW, it seems, had chosen the Compact floorpan/rear suspension for two distinct and closely related reasons. One was that the older-type semi-trailing link rear suspension was much lower than the 'Z-axle' type (more 'compact' in more ways

than one!) – which worked wonders for the packaging of the floorpan behind the seats, and around the boot floor. The other (vital to the 'number crunchers', if not the enthusiasts) was that the 'Z-axle' assembly reputedly cost 50 per cent more to manufacture – which wouldn't do for the Z3, which was meant to be considerably cheaper than other BMWs.

Even though there were mutterings from pundits about the geometry deficiencies in the old-style rear suspension, this was a somewhat over-exaggerated problem. If the E30-style M3 racecar could have been so successful while using this system, there were surely no basic drawbacks? BMW's engineers were clearly still comfortable with this rear suspension, especially as it was known that

The 5-Series of 1988 to 1995 was the forerunner of the E36 3-Series in so many styling cues, as this side-on shot confirms. The 5-Series platform, however, was altogether larger, bulkier, and usually equipped with more massive engines.

Based on the 3-Series Compact platform, early Z3s were available with 1.8-litre or 1.9-litre four-cylinder engines, depending on the territory to be serviced. Although a mid-life facelift changed much of the detail of the car in 1999, all first-generation Z3s shared this same nose style.

By 1999, the Z3 was being offered with a wide choice of engines, one being the silky-smooth 150bhp 24-valve 2.0-litre 'six', and by this time such cars had the wide-hipped tail first seen on 2.8-litre varieties, which considerably enhanced its showroom appeal.

The Z3 tail end, 1999-style, complete with wide wheelarch flares and wide-tread tyres. This car is fitted with the familiar 2.0-litre six-cylinder engine.

much more powerful six-cylinder versions of the car were already being planned (including a 321bhp/3.2-litre Z3 M-type).

The rest of the pressed-steel bodyshell – with a swoopy-style front end, flared wheelarches, prominent sills and two long passenger doors – was conventional enough, and somewhat 'retro' in its shaping. Although BMW did not claim as much, independent stylists sometimes drew comparisons with the legendary (albeit commercially unsuccessful) BMW 507 of the 1950s. The fold-back soft-top had been engineered by the American Sunroof Corporation, and although the seats were unique, the instrument binnacle and facia moulding were obviously closely related to those quite recently introduced in the 3-Series Compact itself.

To students of E36 chassis engineering, the rest of the running gear looked familiar enough, for the entire front suspension, power-assisted rack-and-pinion steering gear, four-wheel disc brakes and the ABS installation were pure 3-Series; as far as the suspension was concerned, compared with the Compact, only the rates and settings had been modified.

The engine line-up, simple at first, would

Choice of four and six-cyclinder engines from 116 to 321bhp

soon become more complicated. At launch there was to be an eight-valve/1,796cc 'four' with 116bhp and (for some markets) a 16-valve/twin-cam/1,895cc 'four' with 140bhp, but within a year the latest 24-valve/twin-cam/2,793cc 'six' would also be added.

By 1999, only three years later, the range of engines on offer was as complex as for almost any other 3-Series derivative, with six different engines (seven ratings) spanning 116bhp/1.9-litres to 321bhp/3.2-

litres. (Naturally, though, there were no diesel options.) All these engines were backed by a five-speed manual gearbox, or in most cases by an optional four-speed or five-speed automatic transmission.

Wider-hipped rear extended to all Z3 models in 1999

Strangely, the mighty M Roadster (which was built in South Carolina) also came with a five-speed gearbox, whereas normal M3s were built with a six-speed transmission.

Nor was that all, for the six-cylinder cars had wider and more bulbous rear wheelarches than the 'fours' at first, and a hardtop coupe version arrived in the autumn of 1998, more of an aggressive sporting hatchback with what could best be described as 'controversial' styling.

During 1999, there was a general reshuffle and update to this entire range, not only by the addition of a 150bhp/2.0-litre 'six' (the sixth different engine in the line-up), but also at the same time by applying the wide-hipped rear end of the original six-cylinder types to all models.

Although some disappointed testers suggested that the Z3 was more 'touring' than 'sporting', and that other two-seaters gave more enjoyment than this, BMW once again seemed to have got this car's marketing stance absolutely right.

As a 'film star' car, the Z3's debut in *Goldeneye* was distinctly damp-squib, for it barely appeared, and certainly did not excel, but the 100,000th Z3 was manufactured in November 1997, only two years after the model's official launch. Although only 2,060 cars were produced in 1995, 46,097 were built in 1996, and 61,015 in 1997. Even though by this time the novelty had worn off, more than 53,000 cars were sold worldwide in 1998, and by the end of the century this model already seemed to be paying back its investment.

5-Series

Digging right back into BMW's heritage, I found that the original 5-Series range came along in 1972 – three years before the launch of the original 3-Series cars. Like the smaller car, this 5-Series range was modified, updated and then replaced at measured intervals – the second-generation 5-Series arriving in 1981, the third-generation in 1988 and the fourth type in 1995.

The two model families which concern me here are the more modern third-generation and fourth-generation types, which not only show that BMW was always adept at thinking corporately and for the long term, but that it had developed component-sharing to a fine art.

Structurally, the 5-Series saloons, which of course have always been physically larger than the equivalent 3-Series, have always leaned more towards the even larger 7-Series types for their style and structural inspiration. Not only that, but the 5-Series cars have always used a larger

and entirely different four-door saloon bodyshell and structure. This is made clear by comparing basic dimensions of the E36 3-Series of 1990 with the new third-generation 5-Series which had been introduced two years earlier:

Model	3-Series (E36 - 1990)	5-Series (3rd gen - 1988)
Wheelbase (in)	106.3	108.7
Front track (in)	55.8	57.9
Rear track (in)	56.3	58.9
Overall length (in)	174.5	185.8
Unladen weight – with 2-litre, 6-cylinder engine (lb)	2,800	3,186
2-litre engine details	150bhp/ 1,991cc	150bhp/ 1,991cc

Most importantly, however, by the early 1990s the two cars had come to share several of the corporate engines and transmissions. A side-by-side study of drivetrains shows that the 5-Series also picked up the same eight-valve 1.8-litre, 24-valve 2.0-litre 'six' and 24-valve 2.5-litre 'six' engines, and the same electronic

Strip away the multi-material glitz (would you have known this car was built in the USA and intended principally for sale in that continent?) and the similarity between the Z3's facia layout and that of the Compact is clear. Even the steering wheel is the same.

The M Roadster was the fiercest of all Z3 derivatives, being fitted with the M3 evolution six-cylinder engines (including a different specification for the USA market), but allied to a five-speed transmission.

The mid-1999 Z3 Roadster not only had style changes at front and rear, but there was also an optional Speedster cover behind the seats, this clearly being inspired by the same type of feature provided on some 1990s-model Porsches.

German sports cars grow wider over the years. Like the Porsche 911, the Z3 started life rather more slim-hipped, but by 1999 it had put on bulk and had grown new-style tail-lamps and wider tyres. This is the very popular 193bhp/2.8-litre six-cylinder version.

engine management systems, along with the same choice of five-speed manual or five-speed automatic transmissions.

When the fourth-generation 5-Series cars were launched in 1995, the relationship between that car and the soon-to-be-launched E46 3-Series types was just as close. The new 5-Series, though physically larger in all respects, shared three six-cylinder engines – the smooth and high-revving 24-valve twin-cam 2.0, 2.5 and 2.8-litre types, and the latest six-cylinder 2.4-litre turbodiesel, plus the same five-speed manual or automatic transmissions as before; the 5-Series would use Steptronic transmission before the same system became available on the 3-Series.

Not only that, but the latest 5-Series had also learned from BMW's favourable

3-Series developments adopted for latest 5-Series models

experience with the E36 3-Series, being the first such 5-Series to adopt power-assisted rack-and-pinion steering, and its own version of the much-praised multi-link independent rear suspension. This was the first 5-Series to use mainly aluminium suspension links, a feature which would also be adopted on the E46 3-Series which was already under development.

There was even a strong visual link between the new 5-Series of 1995 and the E46 3-Series which was to follow in 1998, for both cars used the same type of front-end style – where the bonnet pressing swept forward and down, to surround the famous kidney-shaped grille, and where the quad headlamps were faired in behind a contoured glass cover: even to me, as an E46 owner, it was easy to confuse one type with the other. In styling, the side profile of the two saloons, too, was very similar,

---

Silky six-cylinders

The straight-six cylinder engines used in E36 and E46 3-Series models were the third distinctly different family of 'sixes' put into production at Munich in postwar years.

The original straight-six was a straightforward development of the M10 'four', and was originally revealed in 1968. This big and bulky design was used in BMW's larger models until the mid-1990s, when a new generation of V8s took its place. As with all such BMW engines, it was made in a myriad of forms – single and twin overhead-cam types, 12 and 24-valve, and sizes from 2.8 to 3.8 litres. It was never used in any 3-Series model.

The second straight-six was an all-new 'small' design, the M20, initially built as a 1,990cc unit, then stretched to 2,316cc and finally (in diesel guise) to 2,693cc. Though similar in its general layout to the earlier and larger 'six', it was different in every detail, being a 12-valver with a single-overhead-camshaft cylinder head and belt drive to the camshaft. Announced in 1977, it was used in many 3-Series and 5-Series BMWs during the next decade.

The later, modernized, M60 twin-cam straight-six used in all E36 and E46 3-Series cars was a lineal development of this engine unit, there being many common parts – but because the later engines had chain-driven camshafts and (on some models) single and even double VANOS camshaft timing control, there was a completely different architecture to the cylinder heads.

---

though every single panel and pane of glass was different.

This, of course, is one reason why BMW dealers can cope so admirably with such diverse ranges of car, for under the skin there has always been a surprisingly amount of commonality – something which the technicians find very reassuring.

CHAPTER 8

REBIRTH IN 1998

The E46 saloon

No-one was at all surprised when a new-generation 3-Series saloon – internally coded (and soon known worldwide) as the E46 type – was announced in 1997. Although the E36-type of 3-Series had sold better than any previous BMW of this type and size, its eventual replacement had been rumoured as early as 1995.

The first wild rumours to be dispelled were that BMW had even been thinking of adopting front-wheel drive for its new cars. It is true that an all-new front-wheel-drive platform was designed, built and assessed in the mid-1990s by the BMW engineers, but such a layout was eventually rejected as being outside the character of a BMW of 3-Series size, price and character. This work, however, was not wasted, for some elements of that platform proved to be useful when BMW took control of Rover in 1994, and in due course they were used in the new BMW-inspired Rover 75 of 1998.

Like Mercedes-Benz, BMW had studied front-wheel drive very carefully, especially those cars produced by GM/Opel and Ford (whose upper-class models might be considered as rivals), but BMW chose not to emulate them. Mercedes-Benz, of course, opted for front-wheel drive in its stubby A-Class car – but that was a different proposition altogether, which led to some very debatable and highly controversial results.

It fascinated (and flattered) BMW, incidentally, that when Ford came to design its all-new front-drive Mondeo three years after the E36 3-Series had appeared, the new Ford's facia, instrument panel and controls layout proved to be a straight crib of the E36 3-Series layout! How do I know? For the very good reason that I have owned cars of both types . . .

Innovation and tradition

Although the spy-camera shots which surfaced from 1995 onwards were always accurate, the 'industrial espionage' pundits were hilariously wrong in many ways. Forecasts of all-new four-cylinder engines

Rumours were rife but proved to be wide of the mark

were totally wrong – at least in their timing, for we later learned that BMW was to build a new engine manufacturing plant in England, while forecasts of an early launch of new Compacts, and a later launch of an E46-generation Touring, were also wide of the mark. Reports of the new E46 being much lighter (up to 221lb/100kg lighter, said the most excitable reporters) were also totally wrong – the new car, in

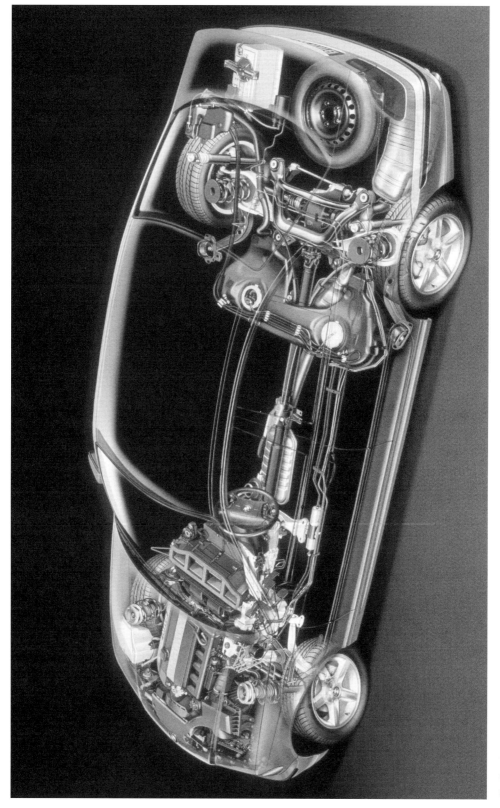

Similar, but by no means the same as before, the E46 saloon of 1998 replaced the E36 model, which had had such a good run. In general terms, the chassis layout was much as before, though there had been a myriad of development changes and improvements.

Although the styling cues were still close, the E46 saloon was different in every line and panel from the E36 which it replaced, the replacement model being slightly longer in the wheelbase, slightly larger, slightly heavier – and even more versatile.

fact, would be substantially *heavier* than before.

A series of design studies and workshop tests of V6 power units had also been made – it should be remembered that BMW already built 90-degree V8 and 60-degree V12 power units, so it was easy to produce prototype V6 derivatives of both types – but as early as 1996 BMW announced that they were not going to be taken any further:

'The study showed', Dr Gerhard Schmidt, director of powertrain development, was quoted, 'that the V6 is preferable to an in-line six *only* if the more compact design is absolutely crucial to the concept of the vehicle . . .' – which, according to BMW's packaging engineers, it most certainly was not.

[Mercedes-Benz, who had just chosen to introduce a new family of V6 and V8 engines, knew that they were being taunted – although not by name – and were apparently not best pleased. In any case, it would not be long before their own strategy would be seen to be flawed, when existing straight-six diesel engines could not be made to fit into the new engine bays which had been fashioned around their own new V6 and V8 power units . . .]

Instead, from a very early stage, BMW elected to make the fourth-generation 3-Series a logical evolution of the best-selling E36 type – slightly larger, slightly heavier, slightly more upmarket, and even more high-tech than ever before. It was a

Saloons first then Coupes, Tourings and the rest in order

strategy with which the entire BMW development team was very comfortable, and it allowed them to produce a magnificently-detailed new model, right out of the box, without teething problems.

The new E46 car was always intended to

The new E46 saloon's interior is a touch more roomy than that of the E36, but even seasoned owners (like the author) have never noticed much difference. Most customers, in any case, like their BMWs compact . . .

For the E46 saloon of 1998, the familiar four-cylinder engine, the M43 type, was only slightly updated to this configuration, this being the 1.9-litre type for the 318i.

be built in saloon, Coupe, Cabriolet, Touring (estate), Compact *and* M3 guises. As ever, not even BMW could launch all derivatives at once, so a rolling programme of launches was decided upon – saloons first, Coupes to follow, Tourings after that, and the rest to follow on early in the 2000s.

Only then would a secondary process of change kick into action. Even by 1998, for instance, it was known that the huge new engine manufacturing factory being erected at Hams Hall, near Birmingham, in

the UK, would produce four-cylinder petrol engines of 1.6 to 2.0 litres capacity, and that these would be fitted to new medium-sized Rover and BMW models from 2000 onwards.

After that, it was said, there would eventually be a new generation of six-cylinder engines, new transmissions, and more, and more, and more. Although BMW certainly did not spell it out, it seemed that the E46 family was destined for a life of at least eight years, if not a full decade, and that its annual production and sales targets were being set even higher than those achieved by the highly successful E36 range.

General layout

Having launched a new-generation 5-Series in 1995, and seen the Z3 Roadster safely onto the market in 1996, BMW was finally ready to show the new-generation 3-Series at the end of 1997. Make no mistake, this had been a mighty design, development and tooling operation, for because the 3-Series was now selling in such huge numbers, it was planned that final assembly should now take place not in

BMW is very proud of its all-new M47 direct-injection four-cylinder diesel engine, which became available in E46 saloons from the spring of 1998. Complete with turbocharging and a big air-to-air intercooler, it was much more powerful than previous BMW four-cylinder diesels, for it produced no less than 136bhp from 1,951cc.

This was the engineering of the new direct-injection M47 diesel for the E46 saloons, complete with four valves per cylinder.

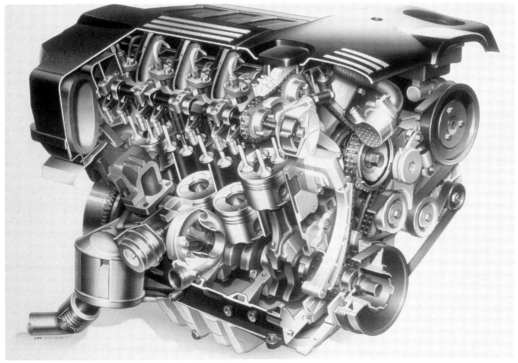

one, nor two, but in four different factories – in Munich, Dingolfing and Regensburg in Germany, plus Rosslyn in South Africa.

The easy and logical way for BMW to describe the E46 model family was as an E36 that had grown up and matured – for although it was slightly larger and a little heavier than before, it still carried many character traits already well-developed by BMW in the 1990s.

Slightly bigger, in fact, meant precisely that, for too much of a stretch would have brought the 3-Series into direct conflict with the 5-Series range. Worldwide, of course, there is a tendency for cars to get bigger over the years, but in this case BMW had had to be extremely careful. The company was already enjoying great success with its latest 5-Series model, which had been launched as recently as 1995, and it was important that its market should not be interfered with by an upgraded 3-Series.

This very simple dimensional chart shows what already existed, and what was decided for the new E46:

Models	E36 (1990-97)	E46 (1997)	5-Series (1995)
Wheelbase (in)	106.3	107.3	111.4
Overall length (in)	174.5	176.0	188.0
Overall width (in)	66.9	68.5	70.9

In addition, the new car was actually 0.9in/23mm taller than before, while front tracks had been stretched by an average of 2.4in/60mm. The overall result was a marginally, but definitely, more capacious car which fitted into only a slightly larger envelope.

Clever packaging and styling by an international team

ZF – automatic specialists

For many years ZF, of Friedrichshafen, in Germany, has been one of the world's leading designers, developers and manufacturers of automotive transmissions, steering gear and other chassis components.

Although quite independent of BMW, ZF has been that company's favoured supplier of automatic transmissions throughout the life of the 3-Series (and other, larger) BMW models. When most manufacturers were happy to use three-speed automatics, ZF was one of the first to offer a four-speed alternative, and by the time the industry was beginning to settle on four-speeders, ZF was already building five-speed automatics.

In more recent years, too, ZF has also developed 'manual-automatics' which, as used in the late-1990s 3-Series types, effectively gave the option of a five-speed manual gearbox with a torque converter instead of a clutch.

As ever, a careful balance had to be struck. For the new-generation 3-Series, BMW wanted to provide more space in the cabin, but a much longer wheelbase would certainly have pushed the new car into 5-Series territory and, according to one insider: 'That would mean the Three would have to be built on the same platform as the Five, and I can promise you we don't have any such plans for that!'

Accordingly, although every single panel was new, the E46 was a model family most recognizably evolved from the E36 variety, and was always destined to be produced in the same cornucopia of types. In some ways it might *look* somewhat like the latest 5-Series cars, but there were no common panels in the two structures.

The new car was the first BMW to be styled under the control of a non-German – American-born Chris Bangle, who had moved across to BMW from Fiat in the mid-1990s – while the exterior styling team was led by a Briton, Ian Cameron.

Critically, in size, bulk and in general marketing stance, the new saloon was very

In many ways the E46 saloon of 1998 used some of the 5-Series styling cues, including the bonnet panel, which swept forward around the famous grille. The whole car was slightly larger and more rounded than before.

From the rear, the way to pick a new E46 from an E36 is to look for the larger tail-lamps, which have sections actually let in to the bootlid. As happens so often on BMW (GB) pictures, the wheels on this particular car, a 328i, are optional extras.

similar indeed in size to the latest Alfa Romeo 156, Audi A4 and Mercedes-Benz C-Class saloons and, as before, there was very little front overhang and a compact tail.

Because the general proportions were much as before, innovation was seen in the details, for example in the way that a 5-Series type of nose was chosen (with a much squatter type of grille) and incorporated in the bonnet pressing, in the headlamps which were matched to rather cute cutouts in the sheet metal under them, and in the L-shaping of the tail-lamps.

There were elements of the 5-Series in the profile of the side windows, but the general shape – low nose, short tail, high bootlid and sharply cut-off tail – were all 'E36-and-more'. Much wind-tunnel testing

(and a wealth of experience) led to the drag coefficient being even lower than before – the smoothest type had a Cd of only 0.27, which was the lowest so far achieved by BMW.

Except that no fewer than four different types of steering wheel were specified (dependent on the model and the equipment specified), along with three trim levels, the interior was familiar to any committed BMW owner. The facia and instrument didsplay might have been all new, but most individual items were updated versions of E36 types. All cars, even the 'entry-level' 316i, were equipped with air conditioning and cast alloy wheels as standard.

Airbags, naturally, figured strongly in the layout, the most fully-equipped version having no fewer than eight bags, including four side/door bags and two long 'sausage' bags on the front screen pillars/above the front doors.

Running gear

Although the E46 models' underbody platform/bodyshell was all new, the new saloon's general 'chassis' layout was clearly an evolution of the E36 variety, complete with the complex rear suspension which had proved to be so effective. The front track, though, had increased by 2.5in/63mm, the rear track by 2.25in/57mm.

In the constant struggle to save weight without losing strength, 50 per cent of the new structure was fabricated in high-strength steel, while many suspension arms and components were now of

Side view of the fourth-generation 3-Series saloon, the E46, confirms that it is slightly bulkier and more rounded than before, with more space in the rear seat. As before, though, there is little front overhang.

Described as having 'seductive' headlamps, with indented metal surrounds and washers hidden away between them, this is a characteristic of the E46 model which would be adopted on other BMW ranges in the years which followed.

Double VANOS – adjustable valve gear on both inlet and exhaust camshafts – had been used on M3s since 1992, but became standard on all six-cylinder engines used in E46 types from 1998. Out of the car, and complete with its transmission, this is an impressive piece of kit, almost all of which is invisible when mounted into the engine bay.

aluminium instead of steel. Four-wheel disc brakes were standard on all types, and both wheel and tyres sizes had increased: 16-inch wheels were standard (and 17in optional) on all six-cylinder-engined cars. BMW claimed a 10 per cent reduction in suspension unsprung weight.

Two other electronic tricks had been finalized, too. ASC+T traction control was now standard (which meant that the driver could not indulge in heroic wheelspinning tactics, as the electronics would not allow this), while CBC (Cornering Brake Control) also individually adjusted front brake caliper pressures if the car began to oversteer under braking.

Once again there had been a reshuffle of the engines line-up, the headline being the arrival of an all-new Type M47 four-cylinder diesel which was not only turbocharged and intercooled, but was equipped with twin overhead camshafts, four valves per cylinder and direct injection. This engine helped BMW to increase diesel-engined sales to 13 per cent of the total.

This is how the new 3-Series engines lined-up in 1998:

316i	1,895cc/4-cyl	105bhp/ohc/8-valve**
318i	1,895cc/4-cyl	118bhp/ohc/8-valve
320D	1,951cc/4-cyl diesel	136bhp/2ohc/16-valve
320i	1,991cc/6-cyl	150bhp/2ohc/24-valve
323i	2,494cc/6-cyl	170bhp/2ohc/24-valve
328i	2,793cc/6-cyl	193bhp/2ohc/24-valve
** This engine was not available until the end of 1998		

– and before the end of 1999:

330d	2,926cc/6-cyl diesel	184bhp/2ohc/24-valve

This, surely, was the final iteration for the existing four-cylinder units, for they were both given twin Lanchester-type rotating balancer shafts, a little more power and torque, and much improved refinement. Compared with the 118bhp engine, the 105bhp unit fitted to the 316i had different camshaft timing and remapped ignition.

Six-cylinder engines now featured steel liners (to help cut down on premature bore

105

Optionally extra, but finding growing acceptance, is this satellite navigation system. This is the E46's console, complete with the optional wooden trim and with the switches for all four electric window lifts on either side of the gear-lever.

The E46 has a larger luggage boot than the E36 which it replaced, but by comparison with several less upmarket rivals it is nothing to boast about! The spare wheel lives out of sight, under the floor, the battery under the black plastic tray behind the right rear wheel.

The facia/instrument display of the new E46 is different in layout from the old E36 variety, but offers the same range of information. Several different airbag-equipped steering wheels are available, this one incorporating controls for (left) the sound equipment and (right) the cruise control.

wear), and were all equipped with the double VANOS adjustable camshaft timing first seen on the M3 Evolution of 1995. Although peak power was not affected, there were significant gains in mid-range torque.

Once again, the choice of transmissions was familiar – five-speed manual gearboxes with different internal ratios, depending on the engine chosen, four-speed and five-speed automatic transmissions, the ZF five-speeders now having Steptronic control.

The author's new E46 328i was equipped with Steptronic automatic. There was conventional automatic transmission with the lever operating in its normal plane: once the lever was in 'D', however, pushing it over to the left meant that it then operated as a clutchless manual gearbox, Touring Car racing change-style, the lever being pushed forward for an upward change, or pulled back for a down change.

A booming business

With the new E46 saloon on the market, with the E46 Coupe expected within a year *(see Chapter 9)*, and other versions already under development, BMW boomed as never before.

In 1998, BMW produced 706,400 cars, which was an all-time record. In the same period, no fewer than 429,900 3-Series of all types (E46 *and* E36) were sold: although the E46 cars only went on sale in April 1998, 146,250 were delivered before the end of the year. The 10-year statistics showed that 3-Series sales had been increasing steadily throughout the 1990s, and with the South African plant now expanded and completely integrated into the manufacturing network there was obvious scope for making even more cars in 2000 and beyond.

With the introduction of the E46 Coupe and Touring models in 1999, BMW clearly had plans to do just that.

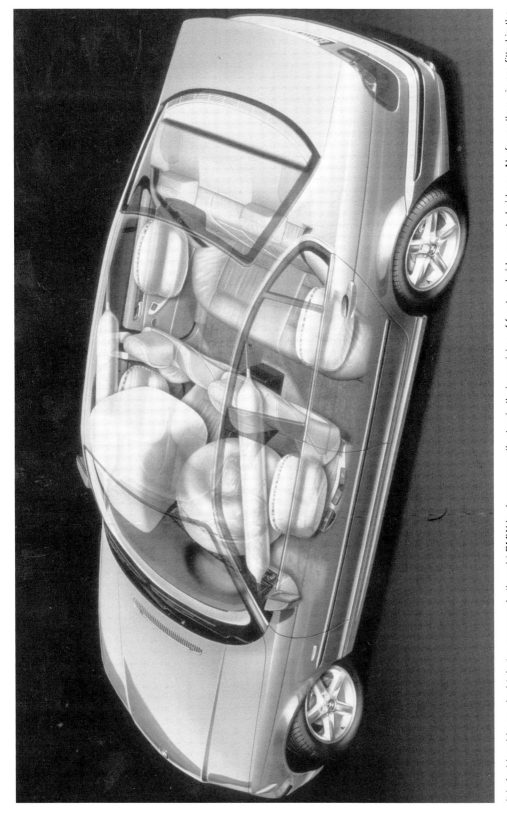

It is fashionable, no doubt, but some people thought BMW had gone over the top in their provision of front and side-mounted airbags. No fewer than six are fitted in the front-seat area alone.

CHAPTER 9

FIRST E46 VARIATIONS

Coupe and Touring

Within months of the introduction of the new-generation E46 3-Series saloon, the range began to expand. First came the arrival of the new-generation diesel engines, which have already been mentioned, and then, within a year, came the smart new range of Coupes.

As with the previous family of Coupes, the new car was unashamedly based on the latest saloon car's platform, and this time the two cars shared absolutely no external panels (though clearly they were related), there being distinctive bumpers and different cooling slat arrangements in the front spoiler. There was virtually no shared exterior hardware either.

the latest car, making sure that everyone noticed the difference by inventing a new system of model naming. While the saloons, of course, were being badged 318i, 323i and 328i (for instance), the new Coupes would always be known as 318Ci, 323Ci and 328Ci.

Sleeker style puts passenger space before luggage room

New naming system chosen to identify E46 Coupe models

Commercially, the new car had a difficult job ahead of it if it was to match the storming success of the E36 Coupe, of which no fewer than 470,000 had been sold in seven years. In some ways, in fact, BMW's top management was a touch defensive about the evolutionary styling of

Although the two-door style was unmistakably sleeker and more sporting than that of the saloons, this was all a matter of degree as the two types were obviously, related, and the same styling cues (headlamps with cowled sheet metal below them, the grille incorporated into the bonnet panel, L-shaped rear lamp/indicator clusters, and seven-spoke alloy wheels, as examples) were all repeated.

As before, of course, the passenger doors were longer than those of the E46 saloon's front doors, their windows were frameless, the rear quarter-windows could be hinged outwards, but not wound down, and there

The new E46-style 3-Series Coupe went on sale early in 1999. As expected, it had a near-identical nose to the saloon, except for the different front spoiler with larger air intakes.

seemed to be a more pronounced tumblehome around the rear quarters which, allied to a prominent bootlid lip, made this new Ci look altogether more lean-hipped than ever.

Yet the new car was undeniably a bit more spacious than before, particularly in the rear seat. The only drawback, however, was that the boot's stowage space had been reduced, though this was not likely to put off many purchasers.

Stiffer suspension and lower roofline enhance sports image

In dimensions, the word 'gradualism' might have been invented for BMW to use, for the differences, though significant,

were also small. Compared with the saloon, the Ci Coupes' windscreen was raked back by a further 2 degrees, the rear window was also subtly flatter and the roof of the car was just 1.8in/46mm lower than that of the saloon. Because the wheelarches were more flared, the overall width, too, was up by a mere 0.7in/18mm.

Sport-type suspension was standard (this lowered the right height by 0.6in/15mm and gave a 10 per cent increase in spring and damper rates, plus beefed-up anti-roll bars), M-Technic settings were soon to be optional, and the gamut of automatic control of braking, stability and traction was all standard. In other words, it was going to be difficult to make a new Ci look untidy, or to feel out of control.

Inside the car the driving seat was lowered, the steering wheel was smaller, and the instruments differently styled. All in all, this was an intriguing package, so subtly and yet definitely different from the saloon, but so obviously based on the layout of that car.

As ever, this was not meant to be just a new car, but a new range of cars, which

110

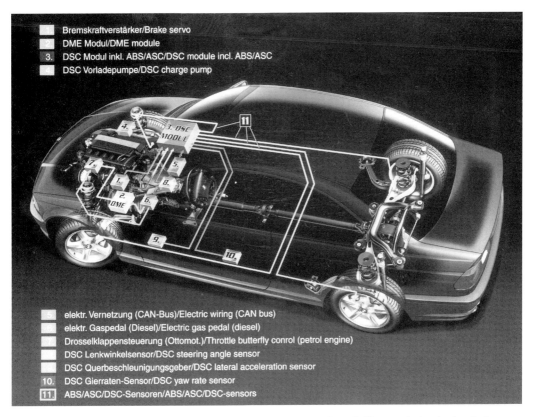

1. Bremskraftverstärker/Brake servo
2. DME Modul/DME module
3. DSC Modul inkl. ABS/ASC/DSC module incl. ABS/ASC
4. DSC Vorladepumpe/DSC charge pump

5. elektr. Vernetzung (CAN-Bus)/Electric wiring (CAN bus)
6. elektr. Gaspedal (Diesel)/Electric gas pedal (diesel)
7. Drosselklappensteuerung (Ottomot.)/Throttle butterfly conrol (petrol engine)
8. DSC Lenkwinkelsensor/DSC steering angle sensor
9. DSC Querbeschleunigungsgeber/DSC lateral acceleration sensor
10. DSC Gierraten-Sensor/DSC yaw rate sensor
11. ABS/ASC/DSC-Sensoren/ABS/ASC/DSC-sensors

Plumbers' and mechanics' nightmare! This drawing shows the number of different electronic circuits incorporated in a 3-series Coupe, all of them connected with ABS braking, traction control and related engine limiters.

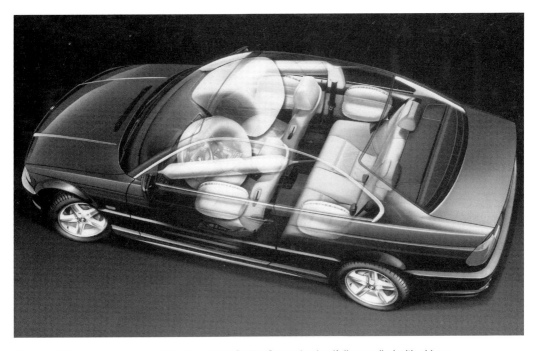

Like the E46 saloon (see page 108), the new 3-Series Coupe is plentifully supplied with airbags.

used many of the recently-revised engines of the E46 saloon. In 1998 the Ci was launched as a trio of six-cylinder-engined cars (320Ci, 323Ci or 328Ci), though an 'entry-level' 318Ci was promised for later in the year. After that, it was supposed, the Ci would benefit from the same new engines which were already being forecast for the four-door saloon. Naturally there was no diesel-engined version, nor was a 105bhp/316Ci proposed, either, for neither car would have had the correct sporting character.

With an immediate choice of 15 exterior colours, 15 different trim options and no fewer than five different types/sizes of wheels and tyres (17in or even 18in wheels, with low-profile rubber) all available, the customer needed to sit down with a catalogue before finally ordering a new Ci –

Except that radios, CDs and satellite navigation equipment vary from individual car to car (depending on what the owner has specified), all E46 saloons and Coupes share the same type of instrument display. This is the plainest of all steering wheels, unfestooned with extra controls or switches.

The only difference between E46 saloons and E46 Coupes (this car) is that the front seats of Coupes can be swung forward to give better access to the rear seats – and of course the doors themselves were significantly longer.

As expected, getting into the rear compartment of a 3-Series Coupe is not easy – and the rear compartment was shaped strictly as a two-seater – but BMW's research showed that these seats were rarely occupied.

Compared with the E46 saloon, the new 3-Series Coupe has much more in the way of air intakes, slots and ducting in the front spoiler. Except for visual impact, there was no immediate engineering need for these, but the M3, when it appeared, would no doubt benefit!

The rear aspect of the new Coupe is almost the same as that of the saloon, except of course for the more sloping line of the rear window. Badged 323Ci, this particular car has the 170bhp/2.5-litre, 24-valve, six-cylinder engine.

and even then he needed to know that BMW's policy of 'continuous development' would probably render it obsolete within a few years!

E46 Touring

As expected, the new Touring made its debut in mid-1999, the only surprise being that BMW had been able to phase it in so soon after the launch of the original E46 saloon. As R&D chief Dr Wolfgang Ziebart admitted when the car was launched:

'The estate car market is far more significant today, so we changed the launch sequence. We've also learned how to ramp up production in a shorter time.' Note that by 1999 he was, at least, permitted to use the phrase 'estate car', even though this car continued to be known officially as a Touring model.

BMW production achievements in the 1990s	
Adding more detail to the way that BMW built up its annual production in the 1990s, total output during the life of the E36/E46 models has been as follows:	1994 573,083
	1995 598,745
	1996 638,341
	1997 669,561
	1998 706,426

Annual production
1989	511,476
1990	519,660
1991	553,230
1992	598,145
1993	532,960

This includes production in South Africa (latterly about 13,000 cars per year) and in the USA (starting in the mid-1990s, more than 50,000 per year). Production at both locations, according to BMW, was to be expanded considerably in the early 2000s.

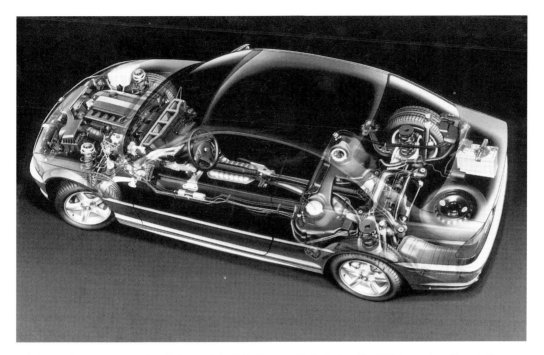

It is interesting to compare the skeleton of the E46 Coupe with that of earlier E36 types, for although the general layout did not change, hundreds, if not thousands, of detail improvements were made along the way. For packaging reasons, note how the fuel tank is really positioned in two volumes, one on each side of the propshaft and well ahead of the rear-wheel line.

The new E46 3-Series Coupe looks handsome from any angle and, as ever, there is no way to pick out the engine of any particular car until one gets a look at the bootlid badge (and even then the owner might have had it removed!). The 17in cast alloy wheels on this particular car were optional extras.

BMW caused a real surprise when they previewed the new-generation E46-style 3-Series Touring in 1999, for the pundits had not been expecting it to be ready for some time. Like other models in this range, the new Touring was no more than an evolutionary step ahead of the previous type which had sold so well in the second half of the 1990s. The seven-spoke alloy wheels fitted to this car were standard (not to say 'basic') equipment on some models, depending on the engine which was fitted.

It was always inevitable that there would be an E46 Touring, because the previous models had been extremely successful. The original E30 type of 1988 to 1995 had sold nearly 104,000 examples, while 130,000 of the E36 (1995 to 1999) variety had followed. Niche vehicles like this, in any case, tend to

Wider rear opening and split rear seat for E46 Touring

be more highly priced, so such programmes must have been very profitable.

Except for equipment detail, the layout of this new five-door car was almost entirely as expected, it being only 1.77in/45mm longer than the previous E36 variety. From the B-pillars forward, the Touring was identical to the saloon, but behind the driver the rear door uppers were squared-off and an elegantly sloping tailgate was added. Predictably, there was a minor increase in drag coefficient – to a Cd of 0.33 – and in weight, but this was still a very effective performer.

Compared with the E36 Touring, there was 65 litres more loading space (BMW claimed a maximum of 47.1cu.ft/1,345 litres), provision of a 2:1 split in the rear seat backrest and – most important – a 4in/100mm increase in the width of the rear opening. The hatchback itself also featured a separate lift-up window glass (as introduced on the earlier 5-Series Touring), and there was a small spoiler built into the top of the hatch.

When deliveries began in October 1999, already there were 318i, 320i, 328i and 320d versions, with a newly-publicized six-cylinder 330d version promised for early 2000.

Four generations of BMW Touring models, showing the latest E46-style model in the foreground. Styling changes at BMW are always evolutionary, as this group confirms.

BMW doesn't like to use the description 'estate car' for its Touring models, but this 2000-model 3-Series looks just like that to us . . .

Although the latest Touring of 1999/2000 is slightly heavier than the saloon on which it is based, it is still a very fast and nimble car. The previous type had sold 130,000 examples in four years, so its future looks promising.

Compared with the E46 saloon, the new Touring has different rear doors and a unique rear structure (which includes a tiny aerodynamic lip over the rear window), but the two cars share near-identical 'chassis' platforms.

BMW did not set out to make the E46 Touring model 'sexy', but merely extremely versatile and practical. There is no badging on this example, but the twin exhaust pipes tell us that a six-cylinder engine is fitted.

And more, and more . . .

BMW, as ever, was not likely to stand pat on new-model development for long, so by the end of 1999, forecasts, promises and strong rumours of additional derivatives were already circulating.

During 2000 the arrival of a new E46 Cabriolet and an E46 Compact looked certain, and the forecast was that the new-generation Compact would use the modern multi-link rear suspension. By the end of the year, a new and extremely exciting M3 (complete with 340bhp/3.4-litre engine) was also promised, though it was thought that no M3 saloon was planned.

Assembly from kits

By the end of the 1990s, BMW was already manufacturing 3-Series cars in five major plants – Munich, Dingolfing, Regensburg, Spartanburg (USA) and Rosslyn (South Africa).

At the same time, CKD (Completely Knocked Down) kits were also being supplied from Germany to Egypt, Indonesia, Malaysia, Mexico, The Philippines, Thailand and Vietnam.

APPENDIX A
3-SERIES INTRODUCTION DATES

Significant new models and derivatives were launched as follows:

E36 range (1990-99 – includes M3, Compact and Z3 models)

December 1990	Introduction of new E36 range of four-door saloons
October 1991	Introduction of new-type 325td diesel-engined model
January 1992	Introduction of E36 two-door Coupe
October 1992	Introduction of new-type M3 two-door Coupe
November 1992	Introduction of new-type Cabriolet
April 1993	Introduction of new-type 325tds (intercooled) diesel-engined models
January 1994	Introduction of M3 Cabriolet
February 1994	Introduction of new Compact hatchback
July 1994	Introduction of M3 four-door saloon
October 1994	Introduction of new 1.7-litre/four-cylinder diesel engine
November 1994	Introduction of E36 five-door Touring (estate) model
February 1995	Introduction of 2.5-litre 323i and 2.8-litre 328i saloons
July 1995	Introduction of M3 Evolution models
November 1995	Introduction of Z3 Roadster (four-cylinder only)
March 1996	Introduction of Z3 2.8-litre version
July 1996	Introduction of 1.9-litre Coupe
	Introduction of facelift and trim changes for four-door models
March 1997	Introduction of Z3 M Roadster
July 1997	Introduction of 323ti Compact
November 1997	Run-out of E36 four-door saloons in favour of new-style E46 model
July 1998	Introduction of Z3 and M Coupe/hatchback
Autumn 1998	Run-out of E36 two-door Coupe in favour of new-style E46 'Ci' models
Winter 1998/99	Run-out of M3 Evolution models
February 1999	Introduction of facelifted Z3 Roadster/Coupe

E46 range (from 1997)

November 1997	Introduction of new-generation four-door saloon
February 1998	Introduction of new-generation 2-litre diesel-engined 320d
November 1998	Introduction of new-generation two-door Coupe
March 1999	Introduction of 'entry-level' 105bhp 316i
May 1999	Introduction of new-generation Touring (estate) model
September 1999	Introduction of 3-litre diesel-engined 330d

APPENDIX B
TECHNICAL SPECIFICATIONS

BMW 3-Series – E36, 4-door saloon/2-door Coupe/5-door Touring/2-door Cabriolet models

Engines:
Petrol:

316i: 4-cyl, iron block, aluminium cylinder head, with single overhead camshaft, two valves per cylinder, 84mm bore x 72mm stroke, 1,596cc. Compression ratio 9.0:1. Bosch/BMW engine management/fuel injection. Maximum power 100bhp (73kW) at 5,500rpm; maximum torque 104lb.ft (141Nm) at 4,250rpm. From autumn 1993, compression ratio 9.7:1, maximum power 102bhp (75kW) at 5,500rpm; maximum torque 110lb.ft (149Nm) at 3,900rpm.

318i: 4-cyl, iron block, aluminium cylinder head, with single overhead camshaft, two valves per cylinder, 84mm bore x 81mm stroke, 1,796cc. Compression ratio 8.8:1. Bosch/BMW engine management/fuel injection. Maximum power 113bhp (83kW) at 5,500rpm; maximum torque 119lb.ft (162Nm) at 4,250rpm. From autumn 1993, compression ratio 9.7:1, maximum power 115bhp (85kW) at 5,500rpm; maximum torque 123lb.ft (168Nm) at 3,900rpm.

318iS (to early 1996): 4-cyl, iron block, aluminium cylinder head, with twin overhead camshafts, four valves per cylinder, 84mm bore x 81mm stroke, 1,796cc. Compression ratio 10.0:1. Bosch/BMW engine management/fuel injection. Maximum power 140bhp (103kW) at 6,000rpm; maximum torque 129lb.ft (175Nm) at 4,500rpm.

318iS (1996 onwards): 4-cyl, iron block, aluminium cylinder head, with twin overhead camshafts, four valves per cylinder, 85mm bore x 83.5mm stroke, 1,895cc. Compression ratio 10.0:1. BMW/Bosch engine management/fuel injection. Maximum power 140bhp (103kW) at 6,000rpm; maximum torque 132lb.ft (180Nm) at 4,300rpm.

320i: 6-cyl, iron block, aluminium cylinder head, with twin overhead camshafts, four valves per cylinder, 80mm bore x 66mm stroke, 1,991cc. Compression ratio 10.5:1. Bosch/BMW engine management/fuel injection. Maximum power 150bhp (110kW) at 5,900rpm; maximum torque 140lb.ft (190Nm) at 4,700rpm.

323i: 6-cyl, iron block, aluminium cylinder head, with twin overhead camshafts, four valves per cylinder, 84mm bore x 75mm stroke, 2,494cc. Compression ratio 10.5:1. Bosch/BMW engine management/fuel injection. Maximum power 170bhp (125kW) at 5,500rpm; maximum torque 181lb.ft (245Nm) at 3,950rpm

325i: 6-cyl, iron block, aluminium cylinder head, with twin overhead camshafts, four valves per cylinder, 84mm bore x 75mm stroke, 2,494cc. Compression ratio 10.0:1. Bosch/BMW engine management/fuel injection. Maximum power 192bhp (141kW) at 5,900rpm; maximum torque 181lb.ft (245Nm) at 4,700rpm.

328i: 6-cyl, aluminium block (iron block, some markets), aluminium cylinder head, with twin overhead camshafts, four valves per cylinder, 84mm bore x 84mm stroke, 2,793cc. Compression ratio 10.2:1. Bosch/BMW engine management/fuel injection. Maximum power 193bhp (142kW) at 5,300rpm; maximum torque 206lb.ft (280Nm) at 3,950rpm.

Diesel:

318tds: 4-cyl, iron block, aluminium cylinder head, with single overhead camshaft, two valves per cylinder, 80mm bore x 82.8mm stroke, 1,665cc. Compression ratio 22.0:1. Bosch/BMW engine management/fuel injection, with turbocharger and intercooler. Maximum power 90bhp (66kW) at 4,400rpm; maximum torque 140lb.ft (190Nm) at 2,000rpm.

325td: 6-cyl, iron block, aluminium cylinder head, with single overhead camshaft, two valves per cylinder, 80mm bore x 82.8mm stroke, 2,498cc. Compression ratio 22.0:1. Bosch/BMW engine management/fuel injection, with turbocharger. Maximum power 115bhp (85kW) at 4,800rpm; maximum torque 163lb.ft (222Nm) at 1,900rpm.

325tds: 6-cyl, iron block, aluminium cylinder head, with single overhead camshaft, two valves per cylinder, 80mm bore x 82.8mm stroke, 2,498cc. Compression ratio 22.0:1. Bosch/BMW engine management/fuel injection, with turbocharger and intercooler. Maximum power 143bhp (105kW) at 4,800rpm; maximum torque 192lb.ft (260Nm) at 2,200rpm.

Transmission:
Front engine/rear drive, with choice of 5-speed all-synchromesh manual, or 5-speed (4-speed, some models) automatic transmission.

Manual:
5-speed manual transmission (internal ratios):

316i, 318i, 320i, 323i and 325i: 4.23, 2.519, 1.665, 1.222, 1.000, reverse 4.039:1.

318tds: 5.43, 2.95, 1.81, 1.26, 1.000, reverse 4.96:1.

325td and 325tds: 5.09, 2.80, 1.76, 1.25, 1.000, reverse 4.71:1.

328i: 4.20, 2.49, 1.66, 1.24, 1.000, reverse 3.89:1.

Automatic:

Automatic transmission, with torque converter (internal ratios):

316i, 318i, 318iS, 325td and 325tds: GM 4-speed: 2.40, 1.466, 1.000, 0.723, reverse 2.00:1.

318iS and 325i – USA market, 325td and 325tds: GM 4-speed: 2.86, 1.62, 1.00, 0.762, reverse 2.00:1.

320i, 323i, 325i, 325td and 325tds: ZF 5-speed: 3.665, 2.00, 1.407, 1.000, 0.742, reverse 4.08:1.

Suspension, steering and brakes:

Ifs, coil springs, MacPherson struts, anti-roll bar, telescopic hydraulic dampers. Irs, coil springs, multi-link control linkage, telescopic hydraulic dampers, anti-roll bar. Power-assisted rack-and-pinion steering. 11.3in (286mm) front disc brakes, 11.0in (280mm) rear drum brakes (316i and 318i), 11.0in (280mm) rear disc brakes (all other models). ABS braking always available (optional on earlier models). Cast alloy wheels, depending on model or market, with 6.0in, 6.5in or 7.0in rims. 185/65-15in tyres (316i, 318i, 318tds and 325td) or 205/60-15in tyres (other models). Local variations for some territories.

Dimensions:

Wheelbase	106.3in (2,700mm)
Front track	55.8in (1,418mm)
Rear track	56.3in (1,431mm)
Overall length	174.5in (4,433mm)
Width	66.9in (1,698mm)
Height	54.8in (1,393mm)
Unladen weight:	Closed cars, from 2,492lb/1,130kg (316i 4-door saloon) to 3,010lb/1,365kg (328i Touring). Cabriolets, from 2,690lb/1,220 (318i Cabriolet) to 3,175lb/1, 440kg (328i Cabriolet).

M3 types – 4-door saloon/2-door Coupe/2-door Cabriolet models

Engines:

1992 to mid-1995 (M3): 6-cyl, iron block, aluminium cylinder head, with twin overhead camshafts, four valves per cylinder, 86mm bore x 85.8mm stroke, 2,990cc. Compression ratio 10.8:1. Bosch/BMW engine management/fuel injection. Maximum power 286bhp (210kW) at 7,000rpm; maximum torque 236lb.ft (320Nm) at 3,600rpm.

[For USA market: Compression ratio 10.5:1. Maximum power 243bhp (179kW) at 6,000rpm; maximum torque 225lb.ft (305Nm) at 4,200rpm.]

From mid-1995 (M3 Evolution): 6-cyl, aluminium block, aluminium cylinder head, with twin overhead camshafts, four valves per cylinder, 86.4mm bore x 91mm stroke, 3,201cc. Compression ratio 11.3:1. Siemens/BMW engine management/fuel injection. Maximum power 321bhp (236kW) at 7,400rpm; maximum torque 258lb.ft (350Nm) at 3,250rpm.

From mid-1995 (M3 Evolution, for USA market): 6-cyl, iron block, aluminium cylinder head, with twin overhead camshafts, four valves per cylinder. 86.4mm bore x 89.6mm stroke, 3,152cc. Compression ratio 10.5:1. Siemens/BMW engine management/fuel injection. Maximum power 243bhp (179kW) at 6,000rpm; maximum torque 236lb.ft (320Nm) at 3,800rpm.

Transmission:

Front engine/rear drive, with 5-speed all-synchromesh (until mid-1995) or 6-speed (from mid-1995) manual transmission, or (from 1996) 5-speed automatic transmission. SMG two-pedal gearchange on manual gearbox from 1997.

Manual:

5-speed manual transmission (internal ratios):
M3, and M3 Evo for USA: 4.20, 2.49, 1.66, 1.26, 1.000, reverse 3.89:1.

6-speed manual transmission (internal ratios):

M3 Evo, non-USA: 4.23, 2.51, 1.67, 1.23, 1.000, 0.83, reverse 3.75:1.

Automatic:

Automatic transmission, with torque converter (internal ratios):

M3 Evo: ZF 5-speed: 3.665, 2.00, 1.407, 1.000, 0.742, reverse 4.08:1.

Suspension, steering and brakes:

Ifs, coil springs, MacPherson struts, anti-roll bar, telescopic hydraulic dampers. Irs, coil springs, multi-link control linkage, telescopic hydraulic dampers, anti-roll bar. Power-assisted rack-and-pinion steering.

12.4in (315mm) front disc brakes, 12.3in (312mm) rear disc brakes (all other models). ABS braking as standard. M3: Cast alloy wheels, with 7.5in rims. 235/40-ZR17in tyres.

M3 Evo: Cast alloy wheels, with 7.5in rims and 225/45-ZR17in tyres (front) and 8.5in rims and 245/40-ZR17in tyres (rear).

Dimensions:

Wheelbase	106.3in (2,700mm)
Front track	55.8in (1,418mm)
Rear track	56.3in (1,431mm)
Overall length	174.5in (4,433mm)
Width	66.9in (1,698mm)
Height (Coupe)	52.6in (1,335mm)

(saloon)   53.7in (1,365mm)

(Cabriolet)   52.8in (1,340mm)

Unladen weight (Coupe)   3,219lb/1,460kg

(saloon)   3,219lb/1,460kg

(Cabriolet)   3,396lb/1,540kg

Compact range

Engines:

Petrol:

316i Compact: 4-cyl, iron block, aluminium cylinder head, with single overhead camshaft, two valves per cylinder, 84mm bore x 72mm stroke, 1,596cc. Compression ratio 9.7:1. Bosch/BMW engine management/fuel injection. Maximum power 102bhp (75kW) at 5,500rpm; maximum torque 110lb.ft (149Nm) at 3,900rpm.

316i Compact (1999 onwards): 4-cyl, iron block, aluminium cylinder head, with single overhead camshaft, two valves per cylinder, 85mm bore x 83.5mm stroke, 1,895cc. Compression ratio 9.7:1. Siemens/BMW engine management/fuel injection. Maximum power 105bhp (77kW) at 5,300rpm; maximum torque 121lb.ft (165Nm) at 2,500rpm.

[Note: A very limited production '316g Compact' version was also available, the 1,895cc engine being powered by LPG gas, and producing a peak of 87bhp.]

318ti Compact (to early 1996): 4-cyl, iron block, aluminium cylinder head, with twin overhead camshafts, four valves per cylinder, 84mm bore x 81mm stroke, 1,796cc. Compression ratio 10.0:1. Bosch/BMW engine management/fuel injection. Maximum power 140bhp (103kW) at 6,000rpm; maximum torque 129lb.ft (175Nm) at 4,500rpm.

318ti Compact (1996 onwards): 4-cyl, iron block, aluminium cylinder head, with twin overhead camshafts, four valves per cylinder, 85mm bore x 83.5mm stroke, 1,895cc. Compression ratio 10.0:1. BMW/Bosch engine management/fuel injection. Maximum power 140bhp (103kW) at 6,000rpm; maximum torque 132lb.ft (180Nm) at 4,300rpm.

323ti Compact: 6-cyl, iron block, aluminium cylinder head, with twin overhead camshafts, four valves per cylinder, 84mm bore x 75mm stroke, 2,494cc. Compression ratio 10.5:1. Siemens/BMW engine management/fuel injection. Maximum power 170bhp (125kW) at 5,500rpm; maximum torque 181lb.ft (245Nm) at 3,950rpm.

Diesel:

318tds Compact: 4-cyl, iron block, aluminium cylinder head, with single overhead camshaft, two valves per cylinder, 80mm bore x 82.8mm stroke, 1,665cc. Compression ratio 22.0:1. Bosch/BMW engine management/fuel injection, with turbocharger and intercooler. Maximum power 90bhp (66kW) at 4,400rpm; maximum torque 140lb.ft (190Nm) at 2,000rpm.

Transmission:

Front engine/rear drive, with choice of 5-speed all-synchromesh manual, or 5-speed (4-speed, some models) automatic transmission.

Manual:

5-speed manual transmission (internal ratios):

All except 318tds Compact: 4.23, 2.519, 1.665, 1.222, 1.000, reverse 4.039:1.

318tds Compact: 5.43, 2.95, 1.81, 1.26, 1.000, reverse 4.96:1.

Automatic:

Automatic transmission, with torque converter (internal ratios):

316i Compact: GM 4-speed: 2.40, 1.466, 1.000, 0.723, reverse 2.00:1.

318ti Compact: GM 4-speed: 2.86, 1.62, 1.00, 0.762, reverse 2.00:1.

323ti Compact: ZF 5-speed: 3.665, 2.00, 1.407, 1.000, 0.742, reverse 4.08:1.

Suspension, steering and brakes:

Ifs, coil springs, MacPherson struts, anti-roll bar, telescopic hydraulic dampers. Irs, coil springs, semi-trailing arms, telescopic hydraulic dampers, anti-roll bar. Power-assisted rack-and-pinion steering.

11.3in (286mm) front disc brakes, 11.0in (280mm) rear drum brakes (1.6-litre 316i only), 11.0in (280mm) rear disc brakes (all other models). ABS braking as standard.

Cast alloy wheels, depending on model or market, with 6.0in, 6.5in or 7.0in rims. 185/65-15in, 205/60-15in or 225/60-16in. tyres, depending on models and local variations for some territories.

Dimensions:

Wheelbase	106.3in (2,700mm)
Front track	55.8in (1,418mm)
Rear track	56.0in (1,423mm)
Overall length	165.7in (4,210mm)
Width	66.9in (1,698mm)
Height	54.8in (1,393mm)
Unladen weight	From 2,514lb/1,140kg (316i Compact) to 3,188lb/1,255kg (323ti Compact)

New E46 generation – 4-door saloon/2-door Coupe/5-door Touring

Engines:

Petrol:

316i: 4-cyl, iron block, aluminium cylinder head, with single overhead camshaft, two valves per cylinder,

85mm bore x 83.5mm stroke, 1,895cc. Compression ratio 9.7:1. Siemens/BMW engine management/fuel injection. Maximum power 105bhp (77kW) at 5,300rpm; maximum torque 121lb.ft (165Nm) at 2,500rpm.

318i and 318Ci: 4-cyl, iron block, aluminium cylinder head, with single overhead camshaft, two valves per cylinder, 85mm bore x 83.5mm stroke, 1,895cc. Compression ratio 9.7:1. Siemens/BMW engine management/fuel injection. Maximum power 118bhp (87kW) at 5,500rpm; maximum torque 132lb.ft (180Nm) at 3,900rpm.

320i and 320Ci: 6-cyl, iron block, aluminium cylinder head, with twin overhead camshafts, four valves per cylinder, 80mm bore x 66mm stroke, 1,991cc. Compression ratio 11.1:1. Siemens/BMW engine management/fuel injection. Maximum power 150bhp (110kW) at 5,900rpm; maximum torque 140lb.ft (190Nm) at 3,500rpm.

323i and 323Ci: 6-cyl, iron block, aluminium cylinder head, with twin overhead camshafts, four valves per cylinder, 84mm bore x 75mm stroke, 2,494cc. Compression ratio 10.5:1. Siemens/BMW engine management/fuel injection. Maximum power 170bhp (125kW) at 5,500rpm; maximum torque 181lb.ft (245Nm) at 3,500rpm.

328i and 328Ci: 6-cyl, aluminium block (iron block, some markets), aluminium cylinder head, with twin overhead camshafts, four valves per cylinder, 84mm bore x 84mm stroke, 2,793cc. Compression ratio 10.2:1. Siemens/BMW engine management/fuel injection. Maximum power 193bhp (142kW) at 5,500rpm; maximum torque 206lb.ft (280Nm) at 3,500rpm.

Diesel:

320d: 4-cyl, iron block, aluminium cylinder head, with single overhead camshaft, two valves per cylinder, 84mm bore x 88mm stroke, 1,951cc. Compression ratio 19.0:1. Siemens/BMW engine management/fuel injection, with turbocharger and intercooler. Maximum power 136bhp (100kW) at 4,000rpm; maximum torque 206lb.ft (280Nm) at 1,750rpm.

330d: 6-cyl, iron block, aluminium cylinder head, with single overhead camshaft, two valves per cylinder, 84mm bore x 88mm stroke, 2,926cc. Compression ratio 18.0:1. Siemens/BMW engine management/fuel injection, with turbocharger and intercooler. Maximum power 184bhp (135kW) at 4,000rpm; maximum torque 287lb.ft. (390Nm) at 1,750rpm.

Transmission:

Front engine/rear drive, with choice of 5-speed all-synchromesh manual, or 5-speed (4-speed, some models) automatic transmission.

Manual:

5-speed manual transmission (internal ratios):

316i, 318i, 320i and 323i: 4.23, 2.519, 1.665, 1.222, 1.000, reverse 4.039:1.

320d: 5.09, 2.80, 1.76, 1.25, 1.000, reverse 4.71:1.

328i: 4.20, 2.49, 1.66, 1.24, 1.000, reverse 3.89:1.

Automatic:

Automatic transmission, with torque converter (internal ratios):

316i and 318i: GM 4-speed: 2.40, 1.466, 1.000, 0.723, reverse 2.00:1.

318Ci: GM 4-speed: 2.86, 1.54, 1.00, 0.70, reverse 2.38:1.

320i, 323i and 328i: ZF 5-speed: 3.665, 2.00, 1.407, 1.000, 0.742, reverse 4.08:1.

Suspension, steering and brakes:

Ifs, coil springs, MacPherson struts, anti-roll bar, telescopic hydraulic dampers. Irs, coil springs, multi-link control linkage, telescopic hydraulic dampers, anti-roll bar. Power-assisted rack-and-pinion steering.

316i, 318i, 320i, 323i and 320d: 11.3in (286mm) front disc brakes, 11.0in (280mm) rear disc brakes. 328i: 11.8in (300mm) front disc brakes, 11.6in (294mm) rear disc brakes. ABS braking standard, all models.

Cast alloy wheels – 316i, 318i and 320d: 6.5in rims, 195/65-HR15in tyres. 318i, 320i, 323i and 328i: 7.0in rims, 205/55-16in tyres. 323Ci and 328Ci: 8.0in rims, 225/45-17in tyres.

Dimensions:

Wheelbase	107.3in (2,725mm)
Front track	58.3in (1,480mm)
Rear track	58.7in (1,490mm)
Overall length	176.0in (4,470mm)
Width	68.5in (1,740mm)
Height	55.9in (1,420mm)
Unladen weight	From 2,833lb/1,285kg (316i 4-door saloon) to 3,076lb/1,395kg (328i 4-door saloon).

APPENDIX C
BMW 3-SERIES PERFORMANCE FIGURES

E36-type 4-door saloons (non-M-Series) – petrol-powered versions

Model	316i	318i	320i	325i	328i
Engine size (cc)	1596	1796	1991	2494	2793
Maximum bhp	100	113	150	192	193
Maximum speed (mph)	120	122	132	141	143
Acceleration (sec):					
0-30mph	3.7	3.2	3.0	2.6	2.3
0-40mph	5.7	5.0	4.7	3.9	3.5
0-50mph	8.2	7.4	6.6	5.3	4.9
0-60mph	11.2	10.2	9.1	7.3	6.4
0-70mph	14.9	13.4	12.0	9.5	8.6
0-80mph	20.4	17.7	15.5	12.0	10.9
0-90mph	26.5	23.0	20.2	15.3	13.7
0-100mph	36.0	30.5	25.9	19.2	17.4
0-110mph	–	–	34.0	24.0	21.9
0-120mph	–	–	–	–	28.1
Standing-start					
1/4-mile (sec)	18.2	17.5	16.9	15.8	15.4
Top gear					
acceleration (sec)					
20-40mph	15.0	12.4	13.1	9.7	10.4
30-50mph	13.6	11.3	12.4	9.4	9.3
40-60mph	13.6	11.4	12.1	9.5	8.9
50-70mph	14.2	12.1	12.4	9.7	9.1
60-80mph	15.1	12.6	12.8	10.2	9.2
70-90mph	15.9	13.3	13.3	10.8	9.3
80-100mph	18.4	15.6	13.7	11.0	9.8
90-110mph	–	–	15.5	11.5	–
100-120mph	–	–	–	13.7	–
Fuel consumption (mpg)					
– overall	27.8	26.6	23.5	26.6	27.3
Kerbside weight (lb)	2765	2778	n/q	2962	2977
Year tested	1991	1993	1991	1991	1995

E36-type 4-door saloons – diesel-powered versions

Model	318 tds	325 td	325 tds
Engine size (cc)	1665	2498	2498
Maximum bhp	90	115	147
Maximum speed (mph)	114	122	134
Acceleration (sec):			
0-30mph	4.0	–	2.9
0-40mph	6.2	–	4.4
0-50mph	9.6	–	6.4
0-60mph	13.5	10.8	8.8
0-70mph	18.6	–	11.7
0-80mph	26.4	–	15.6
0-90mph	35.7	–	20.4
0-100mph	–	35.8	26.3
0-110mph	–	–	35.2
Standing-start 1/4-mile (sec)	19.3	n/q	16.8
Top gear acceleration (sec)			
20-40mph	30.2	–	–
30-50mph	19.1	–	13.1
40-60mph	13.8	–	9.9
50-70mph	14.5	–	8.9
60-80mph	17.1	–	9.2
70-90mph	21.8	–	10.3
80-100mph	–	–	12.6
90-110mph	–	–	15.1
Fuel consumption (MPG)			
– overall	35.8	29.6	31.7
Kerbside weight (lb)	2851	2944	2902
Year tested	1995	1993	1993

E-36 2-door types – M3 and Coupe

Model	318iS Coupe	325I Coupe	M3 Coupe	M3 Cabrio	M3 Evo SMG
Engine size (cc)	1796	2494	2990	2990	3201
Maximum bhp	140	192	286	286	321
Maximum speed (mph)	132	144	162	155	155
Acceleration (sec):					
0-30mph	2.9	2.6	2.2	2.3	1.9
0-40mph	4.7	3.8	3.1	3.3	3.0
0-50mph	6.6	5.4	4.1	4.5	4.2
0-60mph	9.3	7.2	5.4	5.7	5.3
0-70mph	12.2	9.5	6.9	7.4	7.1
0-80mph	15.9	12.0	8.8	9.4	8.7
0-90mph	21.0	15.2	10.8	11.6	10.5
0-100mph	26.8	19.2	13.1	14.3	12.9
0-110mph	35.4	23.8	16.4	–	15.5
0-120mph	–	–	20.0	–	18.4
0-130mph	–	–	25.2	–	–
0-140mph	–	–	30.8	–	–
Standing-start 1/4-mile (sec)	17.0	15.6	13.9	14.4	13.9

Top gear
acceleration (sec)

10-30mph	–	–	9.5	–	–
20-40mph	13.7	9.8	8.1	8.6	–
30-50mph	12.0	9.4	7.3	7.6	9.2
40-60mph	11.3	9.5	8.1	7.3	8.1
50-70mph	11.4	9.6	7.1	7.7	8.2
60-80mph	12.3	9.9	6.0	7.0	8.1
70-90mph	12.7	10.4	6.8	7.4	8.2
80-100mph	13.6	10.7	6.9	–	8.1
90-110mph	17.2	11.4	7.9	–	8.6
100-120mph	–	–	8.3	–	–
110-130mph	–	–	8.5	–	–
120-140mph	–	–	11.4	–	–
Fuel consumption (mpg)					
– overall	28.8	24.9	26.2	22.7	22.8
Kerbside weight (lb)	2703	3043	3352	3484	3330
Year tested	1992	1992	1993	1994	1998

Note: M3 SMG of 1998 had SMG transmission with six forward speeds.

Compact models

Model	316i	318Ti
Engine size (cc)	1596	2796
Maximum bhp	102	140
Maximum speed (mph)	117	128
Acceleration (sec):		
0-30mph	3.2	3.3
0-40mph	5.0	5.1
0-50mph	7.1	7.1
0-60mph	9.9	9.8
0-70mph	13.3	12.0
0-80mph	18.4	16.6
0-90mph	24.8	22.9
0-100mph	34.6	30.7
Standing-start		
1/4-mile (sec)	17.5	17.4
Top gear		
acceleration (sec)		
20-40mph	12.1	13.9
30-50mph	11.3	12.8
40-60mph	12.1	12.7
50-70mph	13.0	13.2
60-80mph	14.1	14.1
70-90mph	15.7	15.7
80-100mph	22.0	18.8
Fuel consumption (mpg)		
– overall	36.3	27.0
Kerbside weight (lb)	2514	2776
Year tested	1994	1994

New-generation (E46) 4-door models – 1998 on

Model	318i	323i	328i
Engine size (cc)	1895	2494	2793
Maximum bhp	118	170	193
Maximum speed (mph)	125	141	148
Acceleration (sec):			
0-30mph	3.2	2.8	3.1
0-40mph	4.9	4.2	4.4
0-50mph	7.1	5.6	5.7
0-60mph	9.6	7.6	7.3
0-70mph	12.9	9.9	9.4
0-80mph	16.8	12.5	11.7
0-90mph	22.3	15.4	14.4
0-100mph	29.0	19.8	18.0
Standing-start			
1/4-mile (sec)	17.3	15.8	15.7
Top gear			
acceleration (sec)			
20-40mph	11.5	10.0	9.6
30-50mph	10.7	9.8	9.1
40-60mph	10.6	9.7	8.3
50-70mph	10.7	9.1	7.8
60-80mph	11.5	9.1	8.2
70-90mph	13.2	9.6	8.6
80-100mph	15.0	10.7	9.3
Fuel consumption (mpg)			
– overall	29.3	23.2	23.7
Kerbside weight (lb)	2844	3193	3175
Year tested	1998	1998	1998